D0816285

Can the REAL JESUS Still Be FOUND?

SIGMUND BROUWER

HARVEST HOUSE PUBLISHERS
Eugene, Oregon 97402

Cover by Left Coast Design, Portland, Oregon

CAN THE REAL JESUS STILL BE FOUND?
Truth Is Out There Series
Copyright © 2000 by Sigmund Brouwer
Published by Harvest House Publishers
Eugene, Oregon 97402

Library of Congress Cataloging-in-Publication Data
Brouwer, Sigmund, 1959–
    Can the real Jesus still be found? / Sigmund Brouwer
    p. cm. — (truth is out there series)
    ISBN 0-7369-0274-0
    1. Jesus Christ—Historicity. 2. Christian life. 3. Generation X—Religious life.
    I. Title.
    BT303.2 .B76 2000
    232—dc21   00-24147

Printed in the United States of America.

00 01 02 03 04 05 06 07 08 09 / BP-PH / 10 9 8 7 6 5 4 3 2 1

To Joey, Keith,
Tyrone, and Tony

Contents

Beginning
Your Search

There is no altar call at the beginning, middle, or end of this book.

It is simply an introduction to Jesus of Nazareth, a man who lived and died in a small Roman province roughly two thousand years ago.

You may have curiosity about this man—as one who believes in his message and resurrection, as a skeptic, or even as someone brought up in a Christian home and expected to follow the footsteps of faith in front of you.

Your curiosity is well justified. No other man has affected the last two thousand years of history as he did. People have died for him. People have killed for him. Millions of people have found peace by trusting in him. Millions of people have transformed their lives by finding a relationship with God through him. Others have rejected him, rejected those who speak of him.

Your curiosity is also gravely important.

If Jesus is who he claimed to be, this has profound implications for your life. If he is not, the implications are equally profound and terrifying for all of those who have placed trust in him.

Jesus and his life and message should at least be considered by everyone who hears of him.

Who was he? Who is he? If you wonder, "What Would Jesus Do," how do you find out what it is he would do in any situation?

I wrote a novel about the life of Jesus, and I found that my upbringing of faith with little knowledge left me at a disadvantage as I tried to answer those questions. This short book of introduction to Jesus arose from the research I did.

Which is not to say that I claim to have all the answers. Hardly. It didn't take much research to discover how much and how often historians differ and disagree in their interpretations of Jesus.

For that reason, it never hurts to reserve judgment on the facts delivered by historians, who at best are secondary sources of information. Because so little is known about Jesus, they must interpret and pass on third-, fourth-, or fifth-party information.

I hope you will rely much more heavily on the primary sources of information about Jesus than on me. These primary sources are the eyewitness accounts of the last years of his life, given to us through the books of Matthew, Mark, Luke, and John. The book of Mark is included at the end of this book, and I would encourage you to read or reread it with this introduction to Jesus.

Objective journalism and objective history writing does not exist. Every writer brings into their work their backgrounds and world perspectives. Accordingly, it would be unfair to pretend this is a coldly objective book. I write it from a platform of faith and trust in Jesus and his resurrection.

On the other hand, I feel strongly that any decision about Jesus you make is yours alone. Only you can decide to have faith. Only you can refuse it. But in order to make a fair decision, it is necessary to know as much as possible about him.

This book, I hope, is a helpful beginning in your search.

TRUTH IS OUT THERE

The
SEARCH

This book began for me at a music-industry party in Nashville, Tennessee. My wife, Cindy, is a songwriter and recording artist, and I was included in the gilt-edged invitation to a glitzy event sponsored by her record company.

The party took place on the thirtieth floor of an expensive hotel as a small part of the Gospel Music Association's huge annual five-day event. Thousands of music artists, aspiring artists, radio people, music-store owners, record company executives, publicity representatives, and concert-booking agents gather for this elaborate extravaganza every year.

I stood at the party in my favorite place, the corner, which serves two purposes. As a writer, I tend to be shy, and a corner position helps keep me out of the main action. Also, as a writer, I like to observe, and a quiet corner gives me the best place for this.

Most of the people at this party were record-company executives, successful business men and women, well dressed, polished in conversation, confident in their place in the world, and especially confident of where they stood in the music world.

As they networked by trading information, jokes, and gossip, my eyes kept going back to four young men in the opposite corner. With their spiked, dyed hair, nose rings, earrings, and Salvation Army grunge clothes, they were conspicuous among the business suits and fifty-dollar haircuts. Conversations flowed around them as if they were a sandbar in a shallow river.

By the shifting of their feet, their crossed arms, and their no-eye-contact glances around the room, it was obvious they knew they stuck out in this crowd. As one of the few nonmusic people in the room, I knew the feeling. On the theory that misery loves company—okay, I was curious—I introduced myself and found out these were the guys from Skypark, a punk music band which had a deal with the record company.

"You listen to any punk?" the guy with green-spiked hair asked. I guessed he thought music would give us common ground for conversation.

"No," I said. For camouflage, I'd gone to this party with the mid-level executive look. "Look at me. Look at my clothes. Look at my hair. Am I the type of person who listens to punk?"

They nodded in understanding.

"What do you listen to?" This from the guy with the shaved head and a ratty, knee-length fake fur coat.

"You don't want to know," I said. "My wife thinks I'm a nerd when it comes to music."

"Country?" he asked.

"Yeah," I said.

"The new stuff isn't that bad," the third guy said. He had massive sideburns and square glasses. "It's got some beat."

"Actually," I said, "the old stuff. The kind where they sing about escaping from jail to learn that their momma ran over the dog in the pickup truck in the rain."

"Oh."

All of us sighed. That ended any chance of a music conversation.

"Is your hair green or yellow?" I asked. "In this light it's hard to tell."

"Green," the spiked-hair guy said. "Neon green. Do you like it?"

"Last week it was orange," the shaved-head guy volunteered. "He does it himself."

"Oh," I said. I couldn't see the hair conversation going much further.

"Right now," I said after a short silence, "you guys look like you'd have more fun poking each others' eyeballs out with a needle."

"This isn't exactly where we do our gigs," the fourth guy said. "I don't think anyone here would like our music."

I asked about their gigs. I learned Skypark drove an ancient, rusty white van with the name of a convent emblazoned on the side, done in theory to deter thieves. They traveled thousands of miles between van breakdowns, and were extremely talented. Although the band members could earn more money staying at home and working regular jobs, they were passionate about using music to share some incredible news with their audiences.

"We see people who are really hurting, man," said one of the band members. He looked kind of like a beatnik, with thick black horn-rimmed glasses. "They're messed up on drugs or come from broken homes and they are desperate for answers. So we tell them about Jesus. And how knowing him turned our lives around."

Jesus.

I slowly looked around the room. At the men in the conservative business suits. At the women who held their drinks just right and laughed in proper tones. Thought about much of the industry talk I'd been hearing all night.

I looked back at these four guys.

It hit me. I laughed.

They gave me a strange look.

"It's funny," I explained. "I think if Jesus walked into this room, he might head right for this corner and talk to you guys first."

"Dude?"

"Think about it," I said, because I was just starting to think about it myself. "He was on the road just like you guys. Didn't care about a regular job, just wanted to pass on his message and help people. He was radical, a rebel."

I paused. "Don't get me wrong guys, but you don't exactly look like establishment material. Neither was Jesus. Most of the establishment hated him, especially when he hung out with the fringe people."

More thoughts hit me. "In fact," I said, "I doubt if Jesus returned today, that he'd be a white, middle-aged, respectable deacon in a respectable church. He just might have a beat-up old van that breaks down on him as he went from town to town."

That observation got the five of us into a great conversation. We talked about a man who suffered constant criticism from the authorities, who reached out to outsiders, who was charismatic and cool, who was rejected by the establishment of his day, who didn't care if he broke senseless rules, who didn't worry about his appearance, whose ideals were more important to him than money, who rocked his world with a radical message, whose story was absolutely amazing, whose life changed world history.

In short, we discussed a Jesus who was not the exclusive property of the congregations of conservative, white, middle-class churches.

Which is not to say he does not belong there. Churches established in the deep faith of his promises truly are his kingdom on earth.

There also churches which do not reflect Jesus or his message, giving those on the outside much to mock or scorn.

Yes, there is much of Christianity that does not reflect Jesus.

There is much of Christianity that does not reflect Jesus.

I once received a large, expensively framed print of Jesus sitting on a bench in a beautiful garden, holding a little boy on his lap. I put this print in storage, where it will remain forever. Why? Well for one thing, nothing appeals to me about a painting of a man holding a boy, surrounded by flowers. Most importantly though, I don't want to add yet another bar to the prison which attempts to hold me back from understanding who Jesus really was.

Jesus.

Think of the word.

Jesus.

Not many words are more recognized or emotionally laden than this one.

Jesus.

Whisper that word and listen to the sound and what it means. Or sing the word. Shout it. Groan it. The word will touch you in as many different ways as you say it.

Jesus.

The word, like the man, rarely leads to a neutral reaction.

Jesus.

Merely a curse word to some. A sergeant in the sky to others. A source of peace. A search of intellectual or historical challenge. Or—oh yeah—the dude on the cross.

Jesus.

Each of us have experiences linked to that word, from devout to atheistic, from joy to fear, from curiosity to boredom. Too often those experiences become prison bars, keeping us away from him.

In childhood, Jesus might have been crayon-colored Sunday school drawings of a man stepping out of the clouds; sentimental paintings of a bearded man with a halo, holding a lamb in his arms; long and boring sermons in a dim church among really old people who sang really old hymns; or it might be memories of messing up lines in a Christmas play as other wise men in white bedsheets stood around a manger lit by fake, flickering candles and gravely looked down on a cheap plastic doll.

As adults, there are other prison bars that separate us from the real Jesus. We watch religious programming where slick con artists use his name to promise healing and prosperity in exchange for sending them our money. Protesters shout the name of Jesus as they self-righteously and hatefully condemn others who don't share their beliefs. Canned music in department stores play his name in Christmas carols during the months-long buying spree that leads up to December 25.

Your doorbell rings, and someone hands you a pamphlet with his name on it. Others who use his name insist the world is only six thousand years old and that fossils were planted by the devil to fool us.

We read historical accounts of Crusaders who raped, pillaged, and killed tens of thousands in the name of Jesus. White supremacists use the name of Jesus as a banner for their cause, unaware or uncaring that he was a Jew. Religious wars are fought in his name. Cult groups use the name of Jesus to suck in the unwary.

And yes, we see him in expensively framed prints: a man in a garden holding a boy on his lap.

Who is Jesus, really?

If you want to step from behind the prison bars which keep you from knowing him, you have to look behind the labels our culture has stuck on his name.

Simply put, he was a celibate Jew with little wealth and formal education who lived two thousand years ago in a dusty, insignificant province which struggled to break free of Roman rule.

There is, of course, more to the answer than that.

But I believe there is a more important question to answer first. A question, once answered, which makes it much easier to understand Jesus and his impact. It is a very simple question.

Before you ask who Jesus is, ask this instead:

Who are you?

Who are you?

In one way, who you are has very little in common with Jesus.

In your world, sports utility vehicles have more technology than the first spaceship to orbit the earth. Technology is changing so fast that your desktop computer has more calculating power than the computers which placed the first men on the moon.

A hundred and fifty years ago, the fastest any human could travel, short of jumping off a cliff, was the speed of a galloping horse. Then came steam engines, internal combustion engines, jet engines. Today, with cell phones and computers, you can instantly communicate through satellites to locations anywhere in the world. Your wealth or potential wealth gives you a heated home with running water, a car, television, washer and dryer—infinitely more luxury than kings who lived only two centuries earlier.

Unlike those kings, you do not store your wealth in gold or silver, but in electronic binary code on magnetic discs in the mainframe computers of bank networks. Your body can be vaccinated, wired, plasticized, and soon, cloned. You entertain yourself with the virtual reality of music videos, computer games, and theater screens three stories tall.

Jesus?

He gripped the road with sandals, not all-weather radials. A full day's travel for him was twenty miles, with the possibility of bandit attack around any turn in the road. He wore his entire wardrobe. His job as a carpenter—until he quit with no unemployment insurance—made him no different than a high-school dropout you might call at random from a yellow pages ad to fix a splintering doorframe. After quitting his job, Jesus wandered homeless from town to town, relying on donations to give him the food to live. As a public speaker, he didn't record any of his teachings, didn't sell books or handouts at his keynote addresses. His followers didn't even take notes; they were too busy hanging out in the same lifestyle.

At first glance, no, you do not have much in common with Jesus.

Yet, in a much more important way, you have everything in common with Jesus.

You are human.

You are human.

You will die.

Far more sad and terrifying is the *knowledge* that you must someday die. Because this knowledge is so sad and terrifying, the easiest way to exist as a human is to avoid thinking of death. We anesthetize ourselves with luxury, television, drugs, and alcohol to live securely in the moment and obliterate this central fact of human existence. Others, however, understand that life is lived more fully with the courage to face death. For it takes courage to love, dream, and build with the certainty that death will eventually remove it all from the earth.

This courage, too, is human.

As is loneliness. To be human means to be separated and alone. Companionship and love ease this loneliness and aloneness; if you are fortunate you will find another person who gives joy to your existence. Yet no matter how close you are to another human, no matter how great your love, it is impossible to merge your being into theirs. You are alone. You will die alone. Many may be gathered at your bedside as you draw your last breath, yet you will be a solitary and tiny figure on that journey through the curtain to whatever lies beyond this life.

As a human, you yearn. It is a feeling impossible to define. You step out of a theater on a warm summer night, filled with the emotions of a wonderful or sad story, and above you is a clear dark night and the brightness of the stars, a backdrop of vastness against the emotions in your heart. Something unknown in you responds to this like a harp string plucked by an invisible hand, and you yearn with a homesickness to be somewhere else, an unknown place as difficult to define as the yearning itself.

Young, you yearn for the future ahead of you, impatient to leave where you are and find where you must go. Old, you yearn for the loves and joys of your past.

As a human, you dream.

You laugh.

You cry.

Hate. Fear.

And most of all, you love.

There are those who believe that because the soul cannot be measured or seen or found through experiment, then humans exist without them. They insist you are merely a complicated package of protein and water, doomed to become dust when your life force fails.

What makes us human, however, is equally invisible and impossible to place in a test tube or on a scale: courage in the face of death, loneliness, yearning, the sources of laughter and tears, dreams, love. What makes us human defies definition without the soul.

Few things in life are simple, but this is one of them: either you have a soul, or you do not.

If you do not, death is an eternal void of darkness, and life's brief dim flash against the span of eternity is next to meaningless. If you do not have a soul, what is there to question? Take what you can in this life. There is nothing else.

If you do have a soul—the essential you which will exist when your body is gone—then comes the awesome mystery of what lies behind the existence of your soul.

Why?

How?

What is beyond this life?

If you have a soul, the purpose of your life is to search for the answers.

The purpose of your life is to search for the answers about your soul.

What you learn will define your actions, your relationships, your goals, your sense of joy and peace. It will be the platform for how you live your life, regardless of the outer trappings of job, geography, wealth, and health.

If you believe you have no soul, then what you learn about Jesus will simply fulfill an intellectual curiosity. After all, it is intriguing that a man who died so young, in such an obscure part of the world and history, could influence billions of people in the twenty centuries which have followed his life and death.

If, however, you believe you have a soul, as part of your search for the truth you cannot ignore Jesus and his message. You may eventually decide not to believe his teachings, his deity, or his resurrection, but you must learn about him to be able to make your decision.

Yet your search cannot begin here. Jesus tells us he was sent into this world by the Creator.

If you believe you have a soul, can you believe it was created by an incomprehensible divine entity who not only brought the universe into being, but loves you and your soul?

God.

Can you believe in the existence of God?

C an you believe in the existence of God?

For the last few centuries, science has essentially told us that God does not exist.

This left thinking people to accept God on the merit of faith alone.

Or to choose the proofs of science without a God.

Not both.

Essentially, this divide began when the Italian scientist Galileo declared that Copernicus' theory was correct: the earth moved around the sun. This directly contradicted the teaching of the church of his day; religious authorities maintained that humans were the central reason for God's creation, therefore, everything, including the sun, revolved around the earth. Galileo was imprisoned for his "sacrilegious" theory.

Ironically, Galileo, a man of deep faith himself, had been attempting to give the church a bridge between statements of faith and the new knowledge yielded by the invention of the telescope. In this case, science was proven right, and the impression among thinking people that the church had a monopoly on truth was lost for all time.

Over the next few centuries, science showed that the mysteries religion had attributed to God all had simple and understandable explanations. Since then, most instances of the church stepping into science has been disastrous for the church. And for a simple reason: The Bible is not a science textbook; it is not a manual of "how," but a manual of "why."

Yet…

Scientists will tell you that the more they discover, the more they discover they don't know.

Physicist Steven Weinberg writes in *The New York Review of Books*: "As we make progress understanding the expanding universe, the problem itself expands, so that the solution always seems to recede from us."

Astronomer Fred Hoyle, with a common sense observation on the big bang theory of the creation of the universe writes: "An explosion in a junkyard does not lead to [assorted] bits of metal being assembled into a useful working machine."

Even the theory of evolution is facing attack within the science community—with scientists at a loss to explain how their fossil records do not show steady change over time, but instead receive mysterious periodic "jolts" of adjustment.

The simple mechanical pictures given us by science since Galileo have begun to be replaced by the understanding that everything around us is incredibly more complex than scientists were once able to imagine—that perhaps this universe is the result of design by a creator, and, even more astounding, that the fifteen-billion-year construction of the universe has had the one goal of producing human life.

Tinker slightly with the fundamental force of gravity, and the universe would either collapse upon itself or disperse into gases; an infinitesimally weaker force at the nuclear level of atoms would make hydrogen—therefore water—nonexistent; decrease the nuclear force by five percent and stars would not exist; an infinitesimally stronger nuclear force would make the creation of protons impossible, giving us a universe of atoms. And so on.[1]

In other words, science and reason no longer stand in the way of a belief in the existence of God.

Still, reason alone will not bring you to God.

Before him, you must be humbled and awed by all the mysteries of existence.

So stop and consider your own life.

Stop and consider your own life. And the world around you.

On one hand, it is preposterous to think that this world is moved by an invisible hand, that something or someone created it and exists beyond what we can sense.

But is it truly preposterous?

After all, life itself is a humbling mystery.

At conception, you were one cell, which contained a nucleus at the center, much like the yolk of an egg. This nucleus contained the microscopic strands of DNA which programmed your growth. Each new cell of the billions which grew to form you in your mother's womb contained the exact copy of the DNA code of the original nucleus, with different strands of DNA programmed to become active as the cells began to specialize. From one cell—sperm and egg combined in a mysterious new spark of life—came the complex organism that is you.

Furthermore, you exist because of sunlight, water, and dirt. Your flesh, blood, and bones are nourished by bread from the wheat which draws from moisture and sunlight and soil; strengthened by the meat of animals which feed upon those plants; sustained by the water which falls from the skies and collects in rivers and lakes.

What an incredible, inconceivable process.

(We are desensitized to this process because we are immersed in it every day. We give it no thought. We order hamburgers at the drive-through window, and they instantly appear in their neatly packaged Styrofoam containers. We stop at the convenience store and buy cold, plastic gallon jugs of milk. We lift the nozzle at the pump, and gas flows into our car. The sun rises and sets; the moon remains in its fixed distance from the earth, held in place by gravity we can predict but not explain.)

If you look at the process of life with fresh eyes, aware of the mysteries, it is not a preposterous notion to think a world with such mystery exists because of the unseen hand of a creator.

You can believe you have a soul.

You can believe you were the result of a creator. God.

But what about that incredibly difficult last step of faith?

Did God become one of us? Did the creator of this universe walk the earth as the man we know as Jesus of Nazareth? Was Jesus divine?

Was Jesus divine?

What a frightening question!

If Jesus was merely a man, the faith of every Christian is meaningless.

If Jesus was more than man, those who reject him also reject God and will suffer eternally for it.

Was Jesus divine?

If you were brought up in a Christian home, where his divinity was never questioned but exalted, you must still answer this question for yourself. You can learn from your parents' faith, but your faith must become your own.

If you were not brought up in a Christian home, and you want the truth about Jesus, there will come a point when you must squarely face this question with all its implications.

Was Jesus divine?

Important as the answer is, in some ways, this can be an unfair and inappropriate question. Too often those who believe in his divinity make this the first issue as they try to pass on his message of hope. Overzealous, they succeed only in alienating, not converting, their audiences. Because it is not the first question about Jesus you should ask or try to answer for anyone, including yourself.

After all, Jesus himself refused to ask or answer the issue of his divinity until it was a fair and appropriate question.

Jesus himself refused to ask or answer the issue of his divinity until it was a fair and appropriate question. Not even to those he called to follow him.

Look instead, in the fifth chapter of his story about Jesus, as Luke recounts the eyewitness report of how Jesus introduced himself to four of the disciples who would travel with him for three years:

> One day as Jesus was preaching on the shore of the Sea of Galilee, great crowds pressed in on him to listen to the word of God. He noticed two empty fishing boats at the water's edge, for the fishermen had left them and were washing their nets. Stepping into one of the boats, Jesus asked Simon, its owner, to push it out into the

water. So he sat in the boat and taught the crowds from there.

When he had finished speaking, he said to Simon, "Now go out where it is deeper and let down your nets, and you will catch many fish."

"Master," Simon replied, "we worked hard all last night and didn't catch a thing. But if you say so, we'll try again."

And this time their nets were so full they began to tear! A shout for help brought their partners in the other boat, and soon both boats were filled with fish and on the verge of sinking.

When Simon Peter realized what had happened, he fell to his knees before Jesus and said, "Oh Lord, please leave me—I'm too much of a sinner to be around you." For he was awestruck by the size of their catch, as were the others with him. His partners, James and John, the sons of Zebedee, were also amazed.

Jesus replied to Simon, "Don't be afraid! From now on you'll be fishing for people!"

And as soon as they landed, they left everything and followed Jesus (Luke 5:1-11).

Simon Peter, Andrew, James, and John had worked through the night, but they couldn't go home to sleep until their nets were cleaned and ready for the next trip out. Their tired, wet hands wrestled with tough cord that cut and sliced their palms and fingers.

Because Jesus spoke to the crowd on the beach from his position in a borrowed boat on the water behind them, the fishermen could not help but overhear his message. Exhausted from working all night and catching nothing, they were not in a frame of mind to be taught. Despite this, the words of Jesus intrigued and impressed them. When Jesus directed Simon Peter to go back out and fish again, Simon Peter didn't tell him to go for a walk, using nonpolite terms learned in the world of fishermen. Simon Peter listened, and he went.

Put yourself in Simon Peter's place. You've been up all night for nothing, and you've just finished the tedious job of cleaning, repairing, and folding your nets. Now a non-fisherman wants you to undo all that work and go out fishing again. As an expert, you know that night is the best time to fish, and there are no fish nearby. Yet because of your respect for this man and his teachings, you go back and try again.

Something incredible happens. Your nets begin to drag with weight, and then to tear. Hearing your shouts for help, a second boat full of fishermen comes out to assist you, but you still can't handle the load of fish.

In awe, you realize your own insignificance compared to this man. You beg him to go away because you realize the gulf that separates you from him. Instead, he asks you to join him. Walking away from the two biggest boatloads of fish and largest one-night paycheck you've ever earned in your life, you give everything up to follow Jesus.

For Simon Peter and the other fishermen, it was a life-changing decision, as it is for anyone who follows Jesus.

Yet they did not make their decision because Jesus walked up to them and informed them he was the Son of God.

No, these fishermen first heard the message of Jesus, and then saw evidence of something supernatural about him. Even then—unlike situations when Christians today try to force their beliefs on others—Jesus did not extend his call until it was obvious, by Simon Peter's plea, that their hearts were ready because of the message and the signs.

They were not ready, however, for the most difficult question of all.

Was Jesus divine?

Once again, we see that Jesus did not unfairly force his friends to decide that before they were ready. As we learn in the sixteenth chapter of Matthew's story, Jesus waited until the end of their three years together—after his closest disciples had witnessed him in action, after they knew him as well as anyone ever could—to directly pose them that question:

> When Jesus came to the region of Caesarea Philippi, he asked his disciples, "Who do people say that the Son of Man is?"
>
> "Well," they replied, "some say John the Baptist, some say Elijah, and others say Jeremiah or one of the other prophets."
>
> Then he asked them, "Who do you say I am?"
>
> Simon Peter answered, "You are the Messiah, the Son of the living God" (Matthew 16:13-16).

Was Jesus divine?

Every person interested in that question should be given the same opportunity to decide as Jesus gave his own disciples. For in a court of law, the judge does not introduce the person on trial and immediately ask the jury to decide the person's innocence or guilt. No, all of the facts are presented, the witnesses are called, the lawyers on each side present their arguments, and only then do the jury members cast their votes.

Was Jesus divine?

You can only answer that for yourself after you learn about the man, his story, and his message. And, as in a court of law, the most important evidence is given by eyewitnesses.

So the place to begin is by going to those who knew and remembered him.

What do these eyewitnesses tell us about Jesus?

What do these eyewitnesses tell us about Jesus?

In one way, very little. All that we know about Jesus essentially comes from the books of Matthew, Mark, Luke, and John, who focus mainly on the time of his ministry. Historians of his time had no reason to pay any attention to him; of his thirty-odd years in an obscure Roman province, he only spent three years in the public limelight, dying as a criminal with no earthly possessions and only a handful of followers.

By the time historians had reason to care about the life of Jesus, it was far too late to retrieve any details of his life. It wasn't until decades after his death that Jesus, through his followers, began to have any impact on the Roman world, which at that time was the only world of importance. And, until the Roman emperor Constantine officially converted to Christianity in A.D. 324 most of that impact was controversial.

As for a record of Jesus' ministry as it happened, Jesus did not write down his teachings, did not keep a journal. Nor did he ask those around him to do so.

In the next third of a century following Jesus' death, his disciples began to spread the word about him, urgently telling listeners about the radical love that he preached, and how the life and death and resurrection of Jesus made his teachings valid. As these original eyewitnesses began to die, it finally became necessary to transmit all of this by written word.

Because this message was spreading so fast and so far, each account of the life of Jesus had a different intended audience, with different emphasis on different aspects of the ministry of Jesus. Conflicting passages among the four accounts do not mean conflicts of truth.

The book of Matthew was written by a Jewish tax collector by the same name whose life was transformed when he met Jesus. Nearly thirty years after Jesus' crucifixion, Matthew wrote his eyewitness account to present a Jewish audience with evidence that Jesus was their long-awaited Messiah.

John Mark was a first-generation follower of Jesus who knew the disciples. He wrote the Gospel of Mark for the Christians in Rome—who were suffering from persecution—to record Jesus' teachings, his work, and his life, and the other three Gospels draw heavily from his material. The Gospel of Mark, written between A.D. 55–65, is probably the first account of Jesus' life ever written.

The book of Luke was written by a Gentile physician who wrote for a non-Jewish audience. Luke's desire was to give an accurate portrayal of the life of Jesus, showing him as a perfect human and perfect Savior.

John, who abandoned his fishing boat that day on the shores of Galilee to follow Jesus, wrote his Gospel last. His intent was to offer evidence to new Christians and searching nonbelievers that Jesus is the Son of God and that through him we can live eternally.

None of these writers felt it necessary to provide the type of historical data you are accustomed to reading in any modern biography. No writers of that time, for that matter, not even the noted Roman writers, pretended to write without bias or interpretation.

The goals of the Gospel writers were not to give a factual, newspaper account of all that happened. They aimed instead to show the eternal importance of Jesus to all lives, the impact and continuing impact of his teachings and deeds, and the truth of his message.

That these Gospels speak to us some twenty centuries later shows how well the writers succeeded in their goals—detailed historical accounts of emperors of that time have been relegated to archives and study books while the story of Jesus continues to touch and transform lives.

Yet to find Jesus, you should at least be able to trust what little is recorded about him.

Which leads to a crucial question.

Are the Gospels reliable sources of information?

Are the Gospels reliable sources of information?

Compared to the immediacy of today's journalism, the three-decade time lapse between the crucifixion of Jesus and the first writings about him seem far too separated to be able to retain any accuracy.

Remember, however, the power of today's media, and the demand it must feed. Remember, too, how recently this phenomena has arrived upon us. While World War II reports reached American newspapers by telegram, fifty years later, the Persian War was broadcast live on television. Two decades earlier, a book took up to a year to go from manuscript to bookstore; books can now be published within days of a major event or released instantly on the Internet. Satellites, telephones, and fax machines have shrunk the world to the size of a village.

In the time of Jesus, the oral tradition of passing along information was much more respected. Readers of the first Gospels would not have had the same reservations or doubts about their accuracy that you might today.

In the Gospels, Jesus is presented with distinct clarity. As a man. As a preacher. As a miracle worker. As a teacher. The stories about him and his deeds are either written directly by eyewitnesses, or have been gathered from them. Because of this, the documents that give witness to the life of Jesus of Nazareth are placed much closer to the beginning events of Christianity than those of any other religious scriptures to their respective origins.

Other religious figures, like Buddha, miss this immediacy by centuries. Buddha died in 480 B.C., and is not presented in writing for another five hundred years. By then he is hardly recognizable as a man, and is seen more as an ideal wisdom type. Confucius, too, filtered by Chinese ideology and the four hundred years that divide him from the writing set down about him, is hardly recognizable as a historical figure. The teachings of the Taoist Way were not formulated in written form until the first century B.C.; the life of the founder, Lao-tse cannot be determined any more precisely than between the fourteenth and sixth centuries B.C.

The immediacy of the Gospels alone, of course, does not give full confirmation of reliability. Today's historians seek second-, third-, and fourth-party sources when determining accuracy. Although little is recorded about Jesus elsewhere, there is enough to be reassuring to those who need the historical data.

For some time scoffers and scholars objected to the accuracy of the description of the burial of Jesus, saying it was common practice of Roman executioners to either leave the bodies of crucified criminals on the cross to be eaten by vultures or throw the bodies into a common grave. The Roman authorities, it was argued, would not have allowed Jesus the private burial described in the Gospels.

This argument collapsed when the skeletal remains of a crucified man was found in a burial cave outside of Jerusalem in 1968. The presence of the victim showed that Roman authorities did permit burial on occasion; the position of the skeleton on the cross, and broken shin bones served as further confirmation of the accuracy of John's description of a normal crucifixion (John 19:32,33).

The contents of another burial chamber in Jerusalem later confirmed more of the Gospels' accuracy when archeologists unearthed the bones of a sixty-year-old man beneath the inscription *Yehosef bar Qayafa*—Joseph, son of Caiaphas. Experts say the remains belong to the man described in the Gospels as the high priest who had Jesus arrested, interrogated Jesus, and gave him to Pontius Pilate for execution (Matthew 26:57–27:2).

The most widely acclaimed confirmation of Gospel accuracy came with an inscribed plaque uncovered near the seaside ruins of a first-century temple in Isreal: "Pontius Pilate, the Prefect of Judea, had dedicated to the people of Caesarea a temple in honor of Tiberius." This is the only known mention of Pilate anywhere in the ancient Roman world and proves the man described in the Gospels indeed had the power ascribed to him—until this discovery, many historians were inclined to doubt Pontius Pilate had ever existed.[2]

Knowing all of this, you may be prepared to accept that the Gospels are accurate eyewitness accounts of the ministry of the man named Jesus. Even so, there are all the "religious" associations that go with the books of Matthew, Mark, Luke, and John.

Because of that, in the search for Jesus, there is a danger in thinking of them as "Gospels."

In the search for Jesus, there is a danger in thinking of Matthew, Mark, Luke, and John as "Gospels."

Through the twenty centuries since Jesus lived, the word "gospel" has taken on new cultural meaning. Through phrases such as "gospel truth," "gospel singing," and "preaching the gospel," we may misunderstand what a "gospel" is.

Gospel literally means "good news."

The Gospels of Matthew, Mark, Luke, and John are real accounts of a real place, written by real people, about real people, for real people. If you come from a Christian background, you may have taken these four books as "gospel truth" for so long that they have lost their significance. If you don't come from a Christian background, the word "gospel" may make you instinctively wary of these "religious stories." Instead, think of the Gospels as a personal introduction to Jesus for you, made by one of his followers.

If you simply think of Matthew, Mark, Luke, and John as personal accounts of time spent with the man named Jesus, it will give you the chance to read about him with fresh, unbiased eyes. Regardless of what you decide about the divinity of Jesus of Nazareth, you will find this witness to his ministry to be compelling and fascinating.

Don't, however, go through the narrations expecting them to read like a modern novel. False expectations may lead you to doubt the realism and truth of these accounts.

False expectations as you read may lead you to doubt the realism and truth of the Gospel accounts.

This danger may not exist for all people—or not even many—but I know it existed for me. I am an avid fiction reader, and because I made the mistake of subconsciously wanting the same story format from the Gospels, too often I relied on faith to help me accept the truth in those accounts.

It wasn't until I wrote a novel, *The Weeping Chamber*, that I discovered how wrong I was in my former approach to the Gospels. The novel is the story of two men during the Passover week leading up to the crucifixion of Jesus. One man needs Jesus and doesn't know it until the end of the novel; the other man, of course, is Jesus.

I had some fear as I began this writing project. The events leading to the crucifixion of Jesus include elements of despair, betrayal, crushing defeat, and the ultimate hope of the empty tomb. I wanted to write this story to the best of my ability. I did not want to make any factual mistakes. I wanted to understand the culture and background of the Jewish life in the first century A.D. I especially wanted to understand the story of Jesus.

My research took me to Israel. I read as much as possible about the history of that time period.[3] I tried to imagine I was there in Jerusalem during that Passover week. I tried to analyze the characters presented in the Gospels and their motivations.

Only then was I ready to begin writing *The Weeping Chamber*.

The first thing I needed to understand was that the novel is a relatively recent invention. Journalism is equally new, and the fast-paced narrative journalism we expect in quality magazine stories has only been around one or two generations.

I also needed to understand that the writers of the Gospels were not unduly concerned with presenting the important events of Jesus ministry in the order in which they happened.

The writers also did not bother explaining things in their everyday life, because most of the first readers of the Gospels already understood the background. (For example, the rituals of the Passover meal.)

And, the writers chose to emphasize different events, and to tell them with different perspectives. For both reasons, compared side by side, an event told in one Gospel may on the surface appear at odds with another.

It may seem minor, but even the presentation of the dialogue of Jesus may seem artificial and contrived if you expect the Gospels to conform with modern form. After all, when you read a novel, no one character speaks nonstop for a half page or more. Jesus, on the other hand, will at times seem to speak endlessly, which may make the presentation of the Gospels seem less realistic. Some Bibles put all of Jesus' words into red: Chapters 14–17 of the book of John, for example, consist almost entirely of red ink.

During the hours I spent reconstructing some Gospel scenes, much of my time and effort was spent comparing and contrasting each scene in the different versions presented by the different Gospels. At first glance, there were contradictions, but upon closer study, especially with the background of everyday Jewish life more clear to me, these events meshed perfectly, leaving me with a sense of awe at the craftsmanship of the writers of the Gospels.

As a novelist, I expected that the issue of dialogue would be the most difficult. It was my goal to use Jesus' words verbatim, as they appeared in the Gospels. My concern was that without altering his words, they would strike a jarring note with readers who were used to the dialogue in popular fiction, not Scripture. Yet again and again, I was struck by how natural his words sounded as I converted each biblical scene into novel form.

After all of this research and study, I realized I did not have to accept the accounts of Matthew, Mark, Luke, and John strictly on faith. I saw, with new eyes, the power and strength of the Gospels. In short, I began writing *The Weeping Chamber* with the intent that my main character would be on a journey to meet and understand Jesus. When I finished the novel, I realized, I too, had been on that same journey.

I met Jesus, the man.

TRUTH IS OUT THERE

The
MAN

The man I met as I wrote my novel does not have a face.

At least not a face I can picture accurately.

If anyone had ever sketched the appearance of Jesus during his time on earth, no images or drawings or sculptures remain; the Gospel accounts give us no clues to his size, the shape of his face, his handsomeness or lack thereof.

I could still form a picture of Jesus in my mind.

It is my guess—and only a guess—that nothing about the appearance of Jesus would have been distracting. It would have hampered his ministry if something about his face—extreme ugliness or extreme handsomeness—would have given listeners a chance to comment among themselves. If he had been noticeably larger than most men, it might have intimidated some, and given others reason to attribute his power, in part, to earthly muscle. If he had been noticeably smaller, he might not have had the stamina to speak for hours on end, to travel on foot day after day after day.

It would be safe to guess that he was in good physical shape. His job as a carpenter would have demanded it; his travel by foot would have maintained this fitness.

Fashion? Again, it is my guess that Jesus did not try to make a statement with extremes. Practicing Jews in his time had long hair, but did not necessarily have beards.

Historical research tells us what most men wore during the time of Jesus. A typical Jewish man wore sandals, an innermost garment, and a sleeved, seamless underdress which covered him down to his feet. This underdress was tied around the middle with a girdle or belt, then covered with a square outer cloth which served as a cloak. Because it was considered a sign of disrespect not to wear a head covering, Jesus probably wore a kerchief twisted into a turban.

Because Jesus was a Jew, and enough of a follower of tradition that for the first part of his ministry he was invited to teach in synagogues, his cloak probably had tassels to fulfill the directives of Numbers 15:38-41 and Deuteronomy 22:12. Tassels served as reminders for a Jew to obey God's commands and be holy unto him. The Pharisees, however, greatly exaggerated the fringes of their cloaks so that everybody could immediately see how righteous they were. Given his teachings and attitudes toward the Pharisees, it is unlikely that Jesus would have done this to his cloak.

No matter how unassuming his appearance was, Jesus stood out from the crowd. When he looked you fully in the face, his inner stillness and total awareness of God would have been penetrating. His peace, humility, and deep sense of purpose would immediately have brought you calmness. You would have wanted this calmness and peace for yourself. Unless you were threatened by it—and then you might choose to avoid him or hate him. Either way, his presence would cause immediate, strong reactions.

It is a blessing that nothing remains to show us exactly how Jesus looked. The danger in a sketch or sculpture would occur as we searched his face for clues to what set him apart. His friends, who wrote the accounts about his life, knew best. What set Jesus apart was the essence of who he was. His words and his actions.

What Jesus said and what Jesus did fill the accounts of Matthew, Mark, Luke, and John, giving us a far truer picture of who he was than any sketch or sculpture.

In short, ignore the paintings of Jesus holding a lamb and look for him in the Gospel narratives. You will be assured of finding someone much more real than sentimental artwork. Someone so attractive and powerful in personality that he changed and changes everyone in contact with him.

From where would such a man come?

Where did Jesus come from?

The friends and followers who bear witness to his ministry did not meet Jesus until he had reached adulthood. When they wanted to write about him after the resurrection, they were much more interested and concerned about him as the risen and living Jesus. For this reason, little is known or written about his childhood.

We do know he spent his childhood and early adult years in the small region of Galilee. His hometown of Nazareth had a population of about two thousand. The town was mainly comprised of square, one- or two-roomed houses crafted of stone and mud bricks, with flat roofs of wooden rafters covered with sticks and branches.

Luke tells us that near the beginning of Jesus' ministry he returned to his boyhood village of Nazareth and "went as usual to the synagogue on the Sabbath" (Luke 4:16), which tells us by implication that Jesus had regularly done so while growing up. This gives us a good base for understanding the years before his ministry.

Whether an elaborate building in larger communities, or a room with benches in tiny villages where nothing more could be afforded, the synagogue in Jesus' time was the gathering place of highest importance in Jewish culture. It was a place of prayer, a place of religious instruction and study, a place to worship.

Jesus spoke knowledgeably of Old Testament Scripture, which suggests he learned well from the rabbis—his teachers—during his religious studies. His parents probably also taught him enough Hebrew to read the Scriptures.

Firstborn sons traditionally followed the craft or profession of their fathers, which in Jesus' case would have been carpentry. Carpenters at this time built everything from houses to furniture, and repaired doors, windows, plows, and yokes. The craft of carpentry was an honorable one which provided a steady income, so Jesus did not grow up poor or in hardship.

This background gave Jesus a blueprint for his ministry. A carpenter must go from job site to job site, for the home does not travel to the carpenter; Jesus later traveled far and wide to reach his audiences. Carpentry demanded efficiency, quality, and practicality; Jesus later gave spiritual advice in the same manner, useful and necessary to any life in any culture. All major construction projects demanded harmony among many types of craftsmen; later Jesus brought together twelve disciples who ranged in extremity from rebel Zealots sworn to overthrow Roman rule to a tax collector who gathered Jewish money for those same hated Romans.

Yet his carpentry background—especially combined with his humble origin—also worked against Jesus.

He was not a religious scholar. Not a priest. Not a member of high political circles. Not a lawyer. Not a scribe.

He was just a regular working guy who chose unemployment because what he believed was much more important than financial security. What he believed also put him in opposition with the religious scholars, priests, aristocrats, lawyers, and scribes. They consistently mocked him because he was an uneducated peasant who dared to correct and criticize them.

It is during times of difficulty, persecution, and conflict that a person's character is revealed. In his opposition to the powerful, elite, political groups, we see the true Jesus.

Yet, the Gospel accounts do not record the first opposition he must have faced.

The Gospel accounts do not record the first opposition he must have faced. The same place it begins for many who have a dream.

At home.

Jesus' teenage years and his first decade of adulthood are not mentioned at all in the Gospels, except to say that he "grew up healthy and strong. He was filled with wisdom beyond his years, and God placed his special favor upon him" (Luke 2:40) and "Jesus grew both in height and in wisdom, and he was loved by God and by all who knew him" (Luke 2:52).

In terms of gossip, Nazareth would have been no different than any other small town. Everyone would have known and had reason to talk about this carpenter, Jesus, living with his mother and siblings. Because everyone would have already known he was different—Jesus had chosen not to marry.

In his culture, this was significant. As descendants of Abraham, devout Jews believed very seriously that they had a moral obligation to produce children. To choose the single life was very uncommon and radical, showing the person had total dedication to his cause.

Yet for years, people would have wondered what cause.

It is almost certain Jesus gave them no clue. Upon his return to Nazareth, as Luke 4:22 tells us, people were amazed at his teachings, asking, "How can this be? Isn't this Joseph's son?"

Obviously, before his return to Nazareth, he had never spoken to them in that way.

Jesus, then, might have had his own internal sense of destiny, but outwardly, for more than ten years in this small town, all he did was work with hammers, chisels, and saws. No wife, no children, no amassing of wealth. To the people of Nazareth, it would have seemed that Jesus was going nowhere.

Unknown to them, at a time when men his age had teenaged children, Jesus was about to choose a new and unpredictable life path.

Imagine then, when, close to his thirtieth birthday, Jesus informs his mother and siblings that he is leaving their home, leaving his job, and leaving Nazareth.

"For what?" they must have asked.

Could he have answered: "The truth is, mother, that I need to bring the people of Israel back to God, and in so doing, save mankind"?

Not likely.

By all accounts, Jesus mostly let his actions speak for themselves—a wise way to live—and spoke immediately before or immediately after the actions which would back his message. With his destined ministry ahead of him, this was not the time to make grandiose promises or predictions to his family, especially after years of quietly working as a carpenter. Whatever answer Jesus gave when he made his shocking announcement at home, it probably was not satisfactory for his mother and siblings.

Nor well received.

As the firstborn, Jesus was leaving a family which likely had no father.

After all, there is significance in the Gospels' silence about Joseph after the beginning of Jesus' ministry. Since it is doubtful that Joseph would leave his family, and equally doubtful he had no interest or curiosity in his firstborn after Jesus began working miracles, the silence of the Gospel accounts in regards to Joseph leaves us the simple conclusion that he died during the years that Jesus was waiting for God's call. (While Mary was probably a young teenager—thirteen or fourteen—when Jesus was born, Joseph was in his late teens or early twenties. When Jesus reached thirty, Joseph would have been around fifty, near the life expectancy for a Jewish peasant in that time, so a natural death would not be unlikely.)

With Joseph dead, Mary, his mother, was also getting old. If she understood Jesus' call well enough to encourage him, she would have also foreseen the dangers. If she did not understand, she would have wondered why after all the years of remaining close by, Jesus suddenly saw a need to abandon her when she might need him most. Either way, she must have questioned his determination.

And his siblings? Would they have been perfectly understanding? Of a brother who had a message to deliver when the rabbis were educated to do the same thing?

In short, following his dream had a price for Jesus.

He could only do it by stirring up gossip, by giving up financial security, and by enduring the doubts of those closest to him.

The Gospel accounts show us a man who is willing to put his ideals ahead of what the world valued.

And that was only the beginning of what he would show us about himself.

Putting his ideals ahead of what the world valued was only the beginning of what he would show us about himself.

Event after event of the Gospel accounts show us Jesus under pressure and how he responded to the problems he faced.

Here's a short list of the people who brought him problems or forced problems upon him: an insane hermit; a blind beggar; an outcast with leprosy; an adulterous woman; the Roman governor; a traitor among his closest friends; children; wealthy men; a mob of soldiers; a hated tax collector; elite religious leaders; fishermen; Jewish government officials.

Jesus faced problems caused by medical emergencies. By the elements. By temptation. By his approaching death.

Event after event, we begin to see how he was as a man.

Jesus included women among his students and followers, when custom dictated women should be denied this simple right.

Jesus struck down rules and regulations that placed human dignity second to the rules and regulations.

Jesus healed when religious leaders told him he should not; Jesus made wine when his mother asked him to help at a wedding party; Jesus stood in public and lectured against the powerful and elite, knowing it would send him to his death.

Jesus was cool under pressure. Witty. Compassionate. Fun. Ironic. Dignified. Determined. Politically smart.

Jesus was a man of love. A man who didn't hesitate to break unnecessary rules. A man who spoke his mind without fear. A man who threw out some of the greatest recorded one-liners in history. "Whoever is without guilt, throw the first stone." "Render to Caesar the things that are Caesar's."

Jesus was not a wimp; he withstood flogging with pieces of bone tied to the end of a leather whip. Jesus was not a pushover; he walked into the great temple and threw over the money tables in his righteous anger.

You will see all of this as you read the accounts.

But not if you approach the Gospels thinking of Jesus as the guy who holds lambs in Sunday school paintings. Or as a curse word. Or as a name shouted again and again during religious television shows. Or as the reason that hateful Christians condemn sinners.

Instead, read the accounts and think of Jesus as a real person. As someone described to you by a friend who was there—which, in essence, sums up the purpose of the Gospels. Use this accurate description of events to imagine you are there, watching and listening.

Read the accounts. Not as something religious that is supposed to be good for you. Not as something you have to accept on faith. Not because it is part of a daily Bible reading that is part of your religious chores.

Read the accounts as a retelling of wonderful, incredible events. As drama. As confrontation. As food for thought. As something that legitimately deserves your curiosity. After all, these four accounts affected the course of world history.

Read the accounts without any preconceived notions or biases.

Read the accounts—you will discover the real Jesus.

Most importantly, you will discover the real Jesus for yourself.

TRUTH·IS·OUT·THERE

The
MESSAGE

You must discover Jesus for yourself. You must also be careful how you let other people form your opinion.

Hundreds of books, including this one, have been written about Jesus. For every book written, thousands more sermons have been preached about Jesus. For every sermon, hundreds of thousands more opinions have been offered by Christians who witness on behalf of Jesus.

Some authors, preachers, friends, or neighbors might have you believe Jesus was a sweet and tender man who wants everyone else to be sweet and tender and nice, just like him. Others will insist he was a man fighting for social revolution. A wise teacher. A man of comfort. A prophet of damnation. And so on. And so on. And so on.

The Gospel accounts will give you many characteristics of Jesus. In this way, he is made real to us.

The danger lies in taking one characteristic and making it the picture of the entire man. Which makes him unreal. A bumper sticker slogan. A stereotype. A caricature.

How can you sum up any person's life in a one-sentence sketch, let alone someone so complex that he changed world history? In today's media-saturated culture, people are frozen for us at a certain moment in their lives: "actor-turned-president" Ronald Reagan; "born-again-NFL'er" Reggie White; "ex-convict" Charles Colson.

It is easy to form Jesus into a mold, simply because there are so few historical facts about him. Authors and preachers and people on the street can easily abuse this freedom—deliberately or unknowingly—by filling in the blanks around those facts and creating a Jesus in the image of their choice.

Their misinterpretation should not become your misinterpretation. Because that Jesus is someone else's Jesus.

Not yours.

Who is your Jesus?

In answering this, you cannot ignore the guidelines and pointers given to you through the Gospels and through the traditions of faith that have been handed down through the centuries. You cannot form your own Jesus for your own convenience, to justify whatever life you want to live.

Jesus clearly shows you how to live with peace and with purpose. By his teachings. By his example.

Who your Jesus is, however, does not stop at your understanding of who he was as a man. It only begins there.

Once you know him, who your Jesus is will be determined by your relationship with him.

Believing in Jesus is not about believing in truths about him. It is about faith and trust in what he has told us. That God exists and loves you. That Jesus became the bridge to reach God. That your awareness and pursuit of God will be the platform of your life.

Placing your faith in Jesus and his message brings him to you the way the gospels do.

Trusting in him helps you find purpose, meaning, and hope, just as if you were among those who listened to him as he spoke in Galilee.

Trusting in him will help you find purpose, meaning, and hope, just as if you were among those who listened to him as he spoke in Galilee.

Simply put, Jesus did this by bringing the radical message that God was a God who loves his people, and to be forgiven of sins, all that one need do is reach toward God to be embraced by God.

In a modern context, the word "sin" comes with a lot of distracting baggage. Some people feel they don't sin because, for the most part, they don't do bad things like murder or steal. Others associate "sin" with physical pleasures. Or with lectures or sermons or threats of hell and damnation. And, nearly always, sin is linked to judgment. It is an unpopular word, popular only when mocked.

Yet sin is the external result of an apartness from God. God has built a yearning into your soul that can only be filled by him. Without God in your life, your soul has an instinctive need to fill the desperation and hurt of lonely emptiness. Money, success, fame—none of these fill that void. Many of the rich and famous lead lives of desperation.

Inherent selfishness dims our awareness of, and connection to, God. Apart from God, you may seek illusions of joy through painkillers like alcohol or addictive drugs that fool users into a spiritual high. Or through casual sex that promises the feeling of love, but leaves behind sadness and rejection. Or through the pursuit of money as a priority over everything else in life.

When you are desperate and hurting, you may lash out to vent your pain, acts instantly regretted. When you are desperate and hurting, you may lie and cheat to hide your desperation. And the lies and cheating only lead to more desperation and pain.

This desperation and pain not only hurts those who bear them, but those around them. These are the results that have been labeled as "sin."

Jesus understood this. With love. With compassion. As a parent aches for a child in pain, for John tells us that Jesus came not to judge the world, but to save it (John 12:47).

When Jesus brought his message, he began to free Jews who had been slaves to laws placed upon them by the religious establishment.

His compassion was a direct contradiction to the harsh, almost hateful judgment of the religious establishment of Matthew's time.

Perhaps the best way to understand this revolutionary love is to look at Matthew himself. For Matthew knew it well. He was one of those Jesus rescued when there was no other hope for him.

Matthew was a tax collector.

Matthew needed rescuing. He was a tax collector.

If you were a Jew living in the time of Jesus, that label spoke volumes about Matthew.

It is difficult to fully appreciate today the importance placed on religion and nationalism in Matthew's society. Tax collectors were guilty of betraying both. In religious terms, any money given to the Roman emperor was seen as tribute to a heathen king instead of tribute to Jehovah God. In nationalistic terms, every penny given to Rome was a reminder of Israel's bondage to a foreign ruler.

Tax collectors were also hated on a personal level. Because they were allowed to keep a certain percentage for themselves, they looked for as many ways as possible to invent reasons for new taxes: on wheels, on axles, on pack animals, on admission to markets, on pedestrians, ships, river crossings, even on mooring at a dock.

Imagine the anger you would feel when, on a thirty-mile journey, you were stopped at every intersection or bridge by a different tax collector who forced you to unload every bag and package on your mules or camels, a tax collector who opened your personal packages, searched them, collected money on the value of the contents, and then walked away, leaving you to repack. Imagine your hatred knowing the tax collector was keeping much of your money for himself, and sending the rest to Rome in defiance to your commitment to God and your country.

Matthew was such a tax collector, a Jew who acted as a direct official of Roman power, with his customhouse located at a landing place for ships at the north end of the Sea of Galilee, where Jesus had based the first part of his ministry.

Ironically, Matthew and Jesus had the same reasons for choosing this location. Not only was it pleasant there in climate and beauty, it was near a major road of commerce from Damascus in the north to the harbor towns east and south. Matthew collected from ships taking advantage of that thoroughfare. Jesus was able to remain in one spot and reach audiences traveling in both directions.

Matthew would have been no stranger, then, to the message and miracles of Jesus. Although his job made him an outcast, reviled, hated, and disrespected by even the lowest classes of Jewish society, Matthew would have overheard the talk about Jesus, perhaps even listened from the edges of the crowds which gathered around the miracle worker.

Yet Matthew would not have dared hope the words of Jesus could apply to him. According to the Jewish laws of religion, no matter how much remorse he might feel, repentance was next to impossible for him and those like him.

In Matthew's world, sinners could never reach God. Not in life. Not in death.

In Matthew's world, sinners could never reach God. Not in life. Not in death.

Imagine a synagogue of Matthew's day, the equivalent of a church for today's Christian. With one difference. Instead of hundreds or thousands of worshipers, where someone like Matthew might slip in the back and sit unnoticed, the worshipers in the synagogue might only number in the dozens, if that. Every face was known, the background of every person subject to gossip and judgment.

In the eyes of the rabbis—the teachers of law—and in the eyes of every person in that synagogue, someone like Matthew was a sinner until he found a way to become righteous in God's eyes. And, as long as Matthew remained a sinner, God would have no part of him.

What incredible loneliness, to be excluded from God, from society.

So how—according to the Jewish leaders—could Matthew get back to God?

Only by becoming righteous, through his own efforts.

This meant, first, by good deeds, of any and all kinds. By fasting—denying himself food as a means of sacrifice to God. By inflicting punishment on himself—wearing hair shirts inside out, dumping ashes on his head, flogging his back with whips. By repaying every person he had cheated. By publicly admitting his wrongdoing. By avoiding all future sins. By reading a certain amount of the Scriptures each day. By serving in the synagogue.

Some sins, however, were so great that no amount of work by the sinner could make him or her right with God. Murder, adultery, and other listed sins meant only the person's death would satisfy God, as long as this death was preceded by confession. Tax collectors, while not deserving of the death sentence, were so far from grace that it was considered nearly impossible for them to earn a way back to God.

Even if Matthew managed to do enough good deeds, fast long enough, damage his body enough, repay enough to everyone he had cheated, confess enough in public, avoid future tax collecting, and read five columns a day in the Scriptures, he still needed to do one last thing to remain right with God.

Something as difficult for all other people of Jesus' day.

Matthew would need to conform with the hundreds of religious laws which were based on the commandments delivered to the Jews by Moses.

Including the incredibly detailed laws of the Sabbath.

The laws of the Sabbath were incredibly detailed.

Moses delivered this command from God to the Jews: "Remember to observe the Sabbath day by keeping it holy. Six days a week are set apart for your daily duties and regular work, but the seventh day is a day of rest dedicated to the LORD your God. On that day, no one in your household may do any kind of work. This includes you, your sons and daughters, your male and female servants, your livestock, and any foreigners living among you" (Exodus 20:8-10).

Over the centuries since that law was first given, rabbinic legal experts had devised an extensive list of what consisted of work on a Sabbath, the time from sundown on Friday evening to sundown on Saturday evening.

For example, carrying any burden was considered work. A burden was defined as anything over the weight of half a fig. Carrying any burden over that weight was breaking the Sabbath. Furthermore, to move half a fig from one place to another on a Sabbath, and to go back to the first spot and move another half fig was also considered work, because both halves added up to more than the defined weight of a legal Sabbath burden. Yet if a person moved a half fig from one spot to another, then picked up that same half fig and transported it to a third place, it *was* allowed, even if it was the equivalent weight of two halves combined.

Nor was it lawful to scrape dirty shoes. They could be touched with oil or water, however, as long as the oil was not added to improve the shoe or sandal by making it softer. (It was a serious debate what a man should do on a Sabbath if the strap of his sandal broke.)

Among other regulations, a righteous Jew was also forbidden to eat an egg laid on the Sabbath, *if* that hen was kept for the purpose of laying eggs, for then it was considered that the hen engaged in work. But if it was a hen kept for fattening, the egg could be eaten because then the hen's action of laying an egg was not work—instead, the egg was considered a part of the hen that had fallen off the bird, no different than feathers or droppings.

If a man's house had caught fire on the Sabbath, it was considered work to attempt to put it out. If a neighbor who was a Gentile attempted to extinguish the flames it was permitted, as long as the Gentile neighbor had not been requested to help but had volunteered without encouragement by the Jew. Furthermore, of the possessions inside a burning house, a Jew could only remove what was essential for food and drink that day; carrying anything else was considered work.

Healing on the Sabbath? A bandage could be applied to a wound only if it was to prevent the wound from getting worse; efforts to *heal* the wound by applying salve or a plaster or any other medical attention must wait until the Sabbath ended. On the Sabbath, a person suffering from a toothache could not gargle with vinegar to relieve the pain. However, if his or her toothbrush was dipped in vinegar, and the toothbrush was used as part of daily hygiene, then it was permitted.

These are just a minor part of the rules of the Sabbath as dictated by the rabbis of the Jewish faith in the time of Jesus. And the rules of the Sabbath were merely one part of the remainder of the rules that God-fearing Jews were to follow to remain righteous with God.

Is it no wonder that Matthew, one of the worst types of sinners, had no chance to be part of God's kingdom?

And is it no wonder that Jesus was welcomed by so many when he told them they could remove the heavy yoke of the burden placed by all these rules?

For what Jesus preached ran in direct opposition to what the religious leaders of his day preached.

Jesus preached glorious freedom.

Jesus preached glorious freedom.

You do not have to make yourself right to be able to approach God, he told his listeners. Instead, if you approach God he will make you right.

This was the light burden Jesus offered then, and offers now. Whatever your past, Jesus said, God loves you. To be forgiven, all you need to do is ask. With this forgiveness, once again, you will be claimed by God as his child.

Think of the rules laid down by the religious leaders faced by Jesus—and faced by Matthew and those like Matthew. Think of Jesus cutting through all those rules and defiantly declaring those religious leaders to be wrong. Think of how Jesus' message must have sounded to Matthew—hated, cursed, totally alone, and without any chance of finding rest for his soul.

You are Matthew, sitting near the lake at your customhouse. You have heard the teachings of Jesus. You have heard about or seen his miracles. You may even have been a witness the day that Jesus called Simon Peter, Andrew, James, and John to be disciples, for the lake is not a large lake, and the fishing boats gather at a landing spot near the place you demand taxes from those who hate you.

It has been a month, maybe two, of hearing and seeing Jesus. Always from a distance, for you are not truly part of your people. In this time something in your heart instinctively knows that Jesus offers you something you need, for although you have more money than you can ever spend, you ache with loneliness and guilt.

Then comes the day you see Jesus in the distance, walking toward your booth along the road near the shoreline of the lake.

You don't dare leave your collection booth to approach Jesus; you know you are not worthy of him. You never leave your booth anyway, because in your booth, you are safely guarded by your official position, and in your booth you don't have to face the rejection that comes in the parts of your life away from it.

Now Jesus' approach has brought him closer to you. You wait for him to do as all others do. Look away to prevent eye contact. Or spit at the ground to express disgust. But Jesus does neither.

He steps off the road and stops at your booth. Perhaps he shakes his cloak free of dust, perhaps asks for some water, which you gladly give. He looks into your eyes and pierces your soul with love. And says two words.

"Follow me."

You cannot speak, you are so surprised. This love. This grace. This forgiveness which erases all that you have become in your apartness from God. You now belong to God. You close your booth and leave it behind. The old hated part of your life is gone and you will never return to it.

From that day on Jesus gives you a new purpose for your talents. You have a pen, and you are a record keeper. You are a keen observer because you have made your living by seeing through all that people attempt in their efforts to dodge taxes. Because of all this, you will write an accurate account of his ministry, and through this account, help all others like you who had no hope without the forgiveness given by Jesus.

Of all the writers of the gospel, you are so conscious of how it feels to be excluded from God that you take special note when Jesus speaks the words that mean so much to you. And you are the only writer to include these words in your account:

Come to me, all of you who are weary and carry heavy burdens, and I will give you rest...

*C*ome to me, all of you who are weary and carry heavy burdens, and I will give you rest. Take my yoke upon you. Let me teach you, because I am humble and gentle, and you will find rest for your souls. For my yoke fits perfectly, and the burden I give you is light *(Matthew 11:28-30).

A yoke in the time of Jesus was a very common tool. It was a wooden crossbar, fitted to be placed across the shoulders of a servant to carry buckets of water on each end. It was also the heavy wooden crossbar linking two load-pulling animals together, each unable to escape from the other or from their burden.

Your own yoke might be the burden of something you have done terribly wrong, hurting yourself or people around you.

Your own yoke might be the excessive demands of irresponsible religious leaders who forget the simple message of God's love that Jesus taught.

Your own yoke might be a heavy weariness in searching for something to fill the emptiness that God wants to fill.

Your own yoke might simply be a yearning to understand how you fit into this world, a yearning for a sense of purpose.

Jesus speaks to you too.

And he meant it so much that he was willing to die for it.

TRUTH IS OUT THERE

The
STORY

His desire for you to come to him and find rest meant so much to him that he was willing to die for it.

Jesus, like everyone of his time, knew how the Romans executed criminals. By crucifixion. He knew, too, about the incredible torture this death placed on those who faced the Roman punishment.

For this is how you die in crucifixion:[4]

You carry your upright beam to the site of execution. At thirty or forty pounds, this lumber is a bearable weight, except you are weak from the blood you have lost to the whips that slashed your back. You would be nearly naked as you walked past jeering crowds.

Perhaps, though, you would not be aware of this pain or agony. Because you know what lies ahead. And the dread of that knowledge far outweighs anything else you feel.

At the place you will die, you watch as soldiers position the upright beam in the ground. They do not care about your fear. They tell jokes. Comment on the crowd. They wiggle the beam back and forth, filling the hole with dirt until it no longer moves. As if they were merely positioning a post for a fence. When they are satisfied, they turn their attention to you.

Another beam is set upon the ground. Nearby are sacks of provisions for the soldiers. They expect to be near the cross for some time, to guard against anyone helping you down. They will eat to satisfy their hunger as you die. They have seen this hundreds of times. Your groans and screams will not dull their appetite.

Now you are forced onto your back. If you resist, they will brutally kick you and slam you with their spears. But they will not kill you. That would be too merciful.

They lay you across the beam with your arms extended. You are grateful for the merciful Jewish tradition that allows a nearby woman to offer you a cup of strong wine mixed with myrrh. You drink it greedily, and the drugged wine begins to deaden your sensations. But when the hammer is lifted, your bladder weakens, perhaps empties, with renewed fear. Your moment has arrived. No amount of myrrh and wine can protect you.

Several long, sharp nails are driven into your left hand, then the right, pinning your arms to the wood. Several hammer blows miss the spike, and shatter bones in your fingers. The soldiers laugh. You know it could be worse. If the executioner had little skill or time, he would simply pound the nails halfway up the flesh of your forearm, confident that eventually your body weight will tear your arms' soft flesh until the bones of your wrist met the nails and arrested the slow agonizing, downward slide of the body.

Now you are secured to the crosspiece, helpless as soldiers use ropes to draw you upward. They bind the crosspiece to the upright with rope or nails. Your feet are barely off the ground.

At this point, however, the soldiers are far from finished. If they leave you hanging in this manner, death will arrive too quickly from the suffocation that results as your body's unsupported weight pulls down against your lungs.

So the soldiers turn your lower body sideways and push the legs upward. They know your large thigh muscles will almost immediately knot and cramp without any prospect of relief that comes from stretching. The soldiers drive spikes through each of the ankles, splintering bone.

You cannot scream, such is the pain. Your brain is flooded with the different agonies from the different parts of your body.

Flies have arrived to settle on your blood and eyes and nose to torment you.

Yet the real pain has not yet begun.

Left alone in this private hell, you will choose the lesser agony of hanging from the nails driven into your hands, simply because it is unbearable to place any weight on the fragmented bones of your ankles. But you begin to suffocate. Your lungs strain for the sweetness of air until your throat rattles against the choking of a diaphragm unable to push for one more gasp.

Your will to live is an unreasoning desperate creature, and ignores your wish to die. You fight for air and push downward on those cramping thigh muscles, pushing your weight on the iron spikes in your ankles. Broken bone grates against broken bone, an unspeakable white-hot knife thrust of pain, a pain that robs you of the very breath you sought.

When you can no longer endure this pain, you sag again, until your lungs suck for air. You push your weight on your ankles. Until your screaming nerves force you to sag yet once more. You alternate between these two agonies, knowing it may take hours and sometimes days, until exhaustion and dehydration finally send you into the black oblivion that is your only hope.

And the entire time you take to die, your body will only be a scant foot or two off the ground that would give you life, if only someone would take you down during those long, endless hours of horror.

This death, Jesus accepted.

He accepted it at the trial in front of Pontius Pilate, declining to speak the simple words that would set him free.

For Pilate did not want to kill Jesus, and tried everything possible to set him free.

What brought both of them to this point of no return?

What brought both Pilate and Jesus to this point of no return?

The hatred of politically motivated Jews.

Not all Jews.

Not even all of the Jews among the religious and wealthy elite.

But enough of them.

During the previous few years to that point, Jesus' teaching ministry had been a direct and ongoing challenge to the religious establishment, who ruled the Jewish masses through fear and legalism.

Jesus had consistently delivered a simple but profoundly radical message: God loves you. You do not have to earn your way into his presence. He will not turn away from you, no matter what your past. All you need do is call out to God, through Jesus. Your past will be forgiven, and you will be accepted. Eternally. Then live your life according to this new found grace.

His religious opponents had no such welcome for sinners.

Time and again, Jesus clashed with pompous, judgmental, self-righteous religious experts who had no compassion or love or sense of God's presence.

These experts had centuries of tradition behind them. They had standing in the community. They had education. They had the power to force nonconformists out of church and social life. They claimed to be the only ones right with God. They had force in numbers. In essence, they ruled Israel without question, even in the shadows of Roman occupation.

Until the arrival of the rebel Jesus.

Jesus was only one man. Uneducated. Without money. Soon enough, barred from the synagogues, cast out of their religious circles.

Was it a fair fight?

Not at all. For the previous three years, out in the provinces away from Jerusalem, Jesus had made them look like the intolerant fools they were.

This conflict came to a climax that final week in Jerusalem.

During the middle of the night before Jesus faced Pilate, they had assembled as men of the Great Sanhedrin, a tribunal ruling body of the Jewish legal system, which had authority on all local matters except capital punishment. Their goal was to vote on Jesus' guilt, then deliver Jesus to Pilate for approval of a death sentence.

Ironically this was an illegal trial. The men who worshipped the law instead of God had to step outside of the law to kill the man sent from God.

A legal trial would have taken place in the temple during the day, where, according to rabbinic law, it was the only site that capital punishment could be pronounced. A legal trial would have allowed Jesus elaborate safeguards during the testimony of witnesses. A legal trial would have not taken place on a Feast Day, unlike this one where the assembled had arrived past midnight on the Passover, a highly unusual and unprecedented occasion for a tribunal gathering.

Nor did Jesus face a fair jury during this illegal trial.

This lone peasant from Galilee had become a threat to the entire spectrum of established religious and political parties: Herodians, who wanted Herod; Pharisees, who followed the letter of the law; and wealthy and elite Sadducees, who did not believe in a resurrection.

The Great Sanhedrin, which was the ruling body of the Jews at that time, drew from the wealthy and the intellectual and the scholarly men from all of these parties. These were the men that Jesus faced the night he was captured.

Why did all these respected men want him dead so badly?

Why did the men of the Great Sanhedrin want him dead so badly?

Their excuse was simple: The popularity of Jesus threatened to spark all the Jews into suicidal rebellion against the Romans.

Their excuse was also mistaken.

When they sent Jesus to Pilate after the night trial, the Roman governor determined that Jesus showed no interest in sparking rebellion against the Romans and did his best to release Jesus. If Pilate did not see a threat, obviously there was none.

No, each of the religious and political parties had hidden agendas when they condemned Jesus to death.

To the Herodians, the more earthly authority Jesus assumed, the less chance that Herod would gain control of Judea.

The Pharisees? Not all Pharisees were ungodly, but the ones most threatened by Jesus were the ones most self-righteous because of their strict adherence to religious law. They taught that God's grace extended only to those who kept the laws and were outraged that Jesus directly contradicted them by teaching of God's mercy. To these Pharisees, the more people who followed Jesus, the more their own authority was undermined.

The Saducees' religious focus was on the administration of the temple in Jerusalem, which made them wealthy through the offerings placed there to God. During Jesus' time, they had considerable religious and political influence. By raging against the money changers in the temple earlier in the week, and because of his great influence with the crowds, Jesus had disrupted their lucrative income from the temple markets.

Normally, these three groups—the Herodians, the Pharisees, the Saducees—were political enemies. They united as temporary and unlikely allies because of Jesus.

Yet it was not uncommon for self-titled prophets to roam the land, speaking to crowds and seeking followers. None of these men—before and after Jesus—managed to become such a threat that the ruling political parties found a need to join forces.

Moreover, in the 1400 years up to the arrival of Jesus, the Jews as a nation had faced death, famine, and dispersion as each rising world power tried to eliminate their defiance and the religion which gave strength to their defiance. The Egyptians, Assyrians, Babylonians, Persians, Romans—military machines of incredible might—all failed in crushing the Jews.

But now, during this Passover week during the rule of Pontius Pilate as Roman governor, the presence of Jesus threatened to destroy this centuries-old religious system.

How could one man succeed where successions of world military powers had failed?

How could one man succeed where successions of world military powers had failed?

From the perspective of Jewish religious leaders, too many people believed this man was or might be the Messiah.

The Anointed One. The Christ.

The glory of the Jewish nation had peaked under the reign of King David hundreds of years earlier. Since that time, their nation had been divided by civil warfare, defeated by foreign armies, and taken away in captivity by the Babylonians.

Scripture told them that someday God would send them a hero to transform their lives. Always, the Jews held hope of the arrival of this promised one, anointed by God to lead them back to glory—their *mashi'ah*, as he was called in Hebrew.

It was especially so in the years of Jesus.

Two decades earlier, after Herod the Great had died, his son Archelaus had ruled so brutally and incompetently that the resulting civil disruption compelled Rome to step in and administrate. Roman rule was hated at the best of times; when Pontius Pilate became governor in A.D. 26, his insensitivity and cruelty worsened the political situation. Throughout the land, the continuous hope for a Messiah grew into a desperate longing.

Many expected the Messiah to be a military leader, much like King David, who would unite them to overthrow Roman rule. Some believed he would be a holy priest who would bring purity to the faith handed down by Moses. And others thought it might be God himself who would find a way to replace corruption with justice and peace.

Into this national longing for a Messiah came Jesus, healing and performing miracles. Rumors began to fly. From prison John the Baptist sent messengers to Jesus to inquire if he was the Messiah. Although he did not deny he was the Messiah, Jesus frequently cautioned those he healed to keep silent, for fear that the mania for a Messiah would interfere with his work.

John 7:25-27 gives us a glimpse of how it was for Jesus: "Some of the people who lived there in Jerusalem said among themselves, 'Isn't this the man they are trying to kill? But here he is, speaking in public, and they say nothing to him. Can it be that our leaders know he really is the Messiah? But how could he be? For we know where this man comes from. When the Messiah comes, he will simply appear; no one will know where he comes from.'"

Even the religious leaders reluctantly entertained the notion: "The Jewish leaders surrounded him and asked, 'How long are you going to keep us in suspense? If you are the Messiah, tell us plainly.' Jesus replied, 'I have already told you, and you don't believe me. The proof is what I do in the name of my Father'" (John 10:24,25).

Yet, as the crucifixion shows, the religious leaders had no intention of embracing Jesus as the Messiah. Because of his teachings and apparently humble background, they wanted nothing to do with him.

Mostly, however, Jesus made it clear he wanted nothing to do with them.

Jesus made it clear he wanted nothing to do with the religious leaders of his day.

After years of proclaiming his radical message in the distant provinces, Jesus arrived without warning and challenged the religious leaders in their religious and political stronghold, Jerusalem. With its great temple, Jerusalem was the pivot around which Judaism revolved, the place Jews believed God met his people on earth.

Jesus made his appearance in Jerusalem at a key moment. Over 100,000 pilgrims arrived yearly for the Passover, when they celebrated the historical escape of the Jewish people from Egypt. Thousands of pilgrims gathered in the massive temple courtyards during this event.

He arrived in Jerusalem on what we refer to today as "Palm Sunday," the Sunday before Passover. Thousands lined the highway into Jerusalem to cheer his entrance into the city. Jesus spoke openly at the temple the next few days to large crowds who marveled at his teaching and the miracles he performed. Despite their hatred for Jesus, the religious authorities took no steps to prevent him from addressing the people.

Perhaps the best way to understand this scenario would be to imagine Russia at the height of the communist era:

A lone figure stands on a soap box in a square in Moscow, in the shadow of the government buildings.

Crowds gather as he proclaims that communism is corrupt, inefficient, and evil.

People look around uneasily as he continues to talk, wondering when the soldiers will arrive to arrest him. Soon, leading government officials leave their posh offices overlooking the square and begin arguing with the man in full view of those assembled. During the course of the debate, the man makes the officials look so stupid that laughter sweeps through the crowd. Humiliated, the officials scurry away to the catcalls and jeers of the crowd.

Tanks arrive with their cannon barrels aimed at the man. He is not intimidated and launches into a ten-minute speech, openly insulting the government officials. The officials back down and send the tanks away.

The crowd in the square spreads the news of what has happened all through Moscow and the rest of Russia. Those who hear of the man's successful defiance have their eyes opened to the horrors of the communist system and lose their fear of this system, engendered through years of dominance.

Essentially, this was the situation in Jerusalem.

Jesus chose a very public location in the building at the center of the power of the religious establishment. Crowds gathered to listen to his radical message. Religious leaders appeared and unsuccessfully tried to trap him in different arguments. With each failure, the crowds were more amazed and delighted. (Read Mark 11:27–12:40 to enjoy these debates as the crowd did.) The temple police finally arrive and wait in the background for the order to arrest this man. Everyone sees the temple police and tension and expectations run high, but the order does not come.

Imagine now that you are one of those religious leaders among the crowds, in front of the temple police that you dare not order against him. Imagine your rage and hatred for Jesus as he continues to publicly defy you:

> The teachers of religious law and the Pharisees.... crush you with impossible religious demands and never lift a finger to help ease the burden.... Everything they do is for show.... How terrible it will be for you teachers of religious law and you Pharisees. Hypocrites! For you won't let others enter the Kingdom of Heaven, and you won't go in yourselves.... you cross land and sea to make one convert, and then you turn him into twice the son of hell as you yourselves are.... Hypocrites! You are so careful to clean the outside of the cup and the dish, but inside you are filthy—full of greed and self-indulgence!... You are like whitewashed tombs—beautiful on the outside but filled on the inside with dead people's bones and all sorts of impurity.... Snakes! Sons of vipers! How will you escape the judgment of hell? (Matthew 23:2-33).

What actions do the religious leaders take to stop this man? Even after Jesus has driven money changers out of the temples, released the sacrificial animals, and effectively stopped the extremely profitable temple market?

Nothing.

Again, think of this from the viewpoint of the once-supreme, arrogant religious leaders. As Jesus speaks, crowds form in the temple. The people begin to question the established teaching they have followed for so long. You become a laughingstock. Your power is considered a joke.

And more and more the people begin to follow Jesus!

Yet they did nothing to stop him. At least not publicly.

If they had taken Jesus, it would have caused the very riots they wanted to prevent.

Jesus, the rebel who claimed to be from God, was too popular.

Jesus, the rebel who claimed to be from God, was too popular.

Roman soldiers constantly surveyed the temple courtyards from a nearby tower. Extra soldiers, in fact, were put on duty in Jerusalem during religious festivals because of the increased likelihood of a Jewish uprising. At the first sign of trouble, these guards were prepared to storm the temple and impose martial law. Had the temple police tried arresting Jesus as he spoke to thousands in the temple, the ensuing riot would have sparked the very rebellion that religious leaders feared. So they captured Jesus at night, in a garden estate outside the city, while he was alone with eleven of his disciples. The twelfth disciple, Judas, led the authorities and Roman soldiers to Jesus for thirty pieces of silver, the traditional price paid for a slave.

While part of Jesus' popularity resulted, of course, from his public defiance of the religious system, the roots of his appeal were much deeper and had been growing in the parched soil of Jewish hopelessness for years—his message of God's love and mercy. It soaked into the soul like cool spring water.

Even his method of teaching showed how much Jesus cared for his audience.

For, from the beginning, people listened to Jesus.

Jesus told great stories—parables—to get his message to his audience.

When you picture Jesus sharing his parables, let your imagination be drawn to his audience.

At the northern shores of the Sea of Galilee long, rolling hills edge the far horizon. Wind ripples the water, then the tall grass. There is the peace of nature's quiet. And near Capernaum, historians tell you, there is a place where the slope forms a perfect amphitheater.

Jesus would have stood at the base of the slope, with hundreds of people sitting in half circles that spread up the hill. His voice would have been carried by the breeze off the water to reach each of them clearly.

His audience? These were hungry people. Not only spiritually, but physically. They traveled by foot for miles to hear him. Many were in poor health, bodies weakened by years of punishing labor. Few were educated. Hardly any could read.

How long would they have sat quietly and listened had Jesus spoke in abstract terms and concepts beyond their grasp? How long if he had not entertained them, engrossed them so deeply that they forgot their aching muscles, tired bones, and grumbling stomachs?

How long would they have remained had Jesus begun to lecture them until they began to squirm? How long if he had preached at them in the way of their synagogue teachers who burdened them with hundreds of rules?

Jesus did not speak of God or religion in his recorded parables. Instead, he reached these poor, hungry people with stories that held their attention, stories that involved their emotions, and stories that had the impact of strong but simple points.

Yet there was more to the popularity of Jesus than that.

Great storytellers do not receive the crown of Messiah. Great storytellers are not capable of threatening an entire religious system. Great storytellers do not face crucifixion.

There was one other element that made Jesus so dangerous that only death would stop him.

Jesus healed.

J esus was a healer.

He performed miracles.

This is what gave his teachings and claims the power that was so threatening.

The Gospel accounts are filled with stories of the miracles of Jesus and the people he healed. According to the eyewitnesses who tell us his story, Jesus gave sight to the blind and restored hearing to the deaf. He cured lepers. Healed by touch or merely by his word. Jesus raised the dead.

Despite the passage of twenty centuries, his miracles and healings have lost none of their power to threaten those who hear of them.

For it is one or the other.

Either the miracles and healings occurred, or they did not.

If they did occur, it is so beyond the realm of the natural that the implications are as frightening to anyone today as they were to the religious authorities who conspired to kill Jesus.

If they did not occur, Jesus was not the person he, or his disciples, or his followers over the next twenty centuries, have claimed him to be. If they did not occur, then the religious authorities were justified by their code in killing him as a fraud, as an insane man who claimed to be God on earth.

How do you decide whether to believe the accounts of the Gospel witnesses?

Realize first that the passage of distance and time does not make any difference in the credibility of a witness. When you read the Gospels, the writers give you their stories as if they are standing beside you, recounting something they saw only yesterday.

Understand too that some people will deny a miracle even if they witness it with their own eyes. They will come up with some excuse, any excuse, in their determined disbelief to transform what is miraculous into something merely natural.

And understand that there are those who see miracles in anything, and in their eagerness to transform a natural event into the miraculous, allow truth to become lost somewhere in the confusion.

Even today, doctors can talk of a miracle occurring, and prove that a man lived when he should have died. Will you choose to believe it was a miracle, an intervention by God? Or will you believe there must be a natural explanation for it?

In essence, as with any decision which relies on witnesses, it comes down to a matter of belief.

Can you believe a person on the stand in a court of law?

Can you believe the writers of the Gospels? Because this belief requires trust, and trust is nothing but faith.

If you need proof, you will never get it.

Ask yourself, however, if a Jesus without miracles or healings would have had the power, authority, and popularity that made such him a threat to their religious system.

And remember how badly the religious authorities wanted to kill Jesus.

Because miracles and healings were only the beginning.

It was the events which followed his death that gave his message the power to change the world.

TRUTH IS OUT THERE

The
RESURRECTION

It was the events which followed his death that gave his message the power to change the world.

One of the amazing things about the message of Jesus is that it survived, then spread. After all, before the final days before his crucifixion, many of his followers had left him. John tells us that near the end of his ministry, Jesus taught a shocking message: "All who eat my flesh and drink my blood remain in me, and I in them" (John 6:56). Jesus did not mean it in a literal sense, of course, but wanted his listeners to understand that his life had to become theirs, and their lives his.

Jesus said this because many followed him for the wrong reasons. Through his miracles and charisma, he drew many who believed he would become the next great ruler of Israel. Jesus wanted his audience to understand his spiritual mission was the one of importance. Only those who understood that and were willing to accept this difficult teaching remained.

Then, as he began his final journey toward Jerusalem, it became apparent that it was physically dangerous to be identified with Jesus and his cause. The religious authorities had decided that Jesus must be killed; Herod, the king, was also interested in interrogating this rebel. More of his followers decided not to risk association with Jesus.

During the last days before his death, Jesus essentially had only his core group of twelve disciples left. On the night he was arrested, Judas betrayed him, Peter publicly denied knowing him, and the rest of the disciples fled, fearful that they too would be arrested.

Jesus faced death virtually alone, with only a few followers who lingered at the foot of the cross as he was crucified. Publicly tortured and humiliated, it seemed as though his message and teachings would also end at the cross.

Yet from that point—ground zero—his gift of hope rapidly spread into the entire known world. Then, like fire touched to dry grass, it leapt from one generation to the next, so that the life of Jesus had more impact on this world than any person in history.

What happened?

Nothing short of a miracle.

This miracle occurred when his disciples arrived at an empty tomb. When Jesus met them later, after his crucifixion.

Jesus was alive, risen from the dead.

His appearance validated his predictions, his claims, and his message.

The disciples were transformed in purpose. Before the crucifixion, Jesus' teachings were simply radical and almost revolutionary. After the empty tomb, his teachings had eternal significance.

The disciples were also transformed in character. Before the crucifixion, they had fled into the night at the first sign of danger. After the empty tomb, they were lions of courage, uncaring of threats or arrest or death. Their joy, and the hope they carried, took the gospel far beyond the borders of their tiny country.

Any other time in history, however, and they would not have had this opportunity.

Coincidence or divine timing? The Roman empire, with its common language, excellent transportation and communication networks, relative political stability, and expansive coverage of known civilization, provided the ideal climate in history for the news of Jesus to spread. In less than sixty years, the message of Christianity had penetrated all of the Roman world.

If Jesus would have entered the world a few decades earlier, he would have been born into a country rocked with internal fighting. If he would have been born a few decades later, Jerusalem would have been destroyed, and the Jewish revolt against the Romans would have made it impossible for him to travel and teach. A scant fifty years after this, and Israel as a nation ceased to exist; the Jews were dead or dispersed.

The spread of Jesus' message is even more remarkable because of how the circumstances of his death would have been perceived by audiences of the first century.

The foundation of this gospel was that Jesus' death on a cross led to his resurrection on the third day. While it is, of course, the same foundation for the gospel today, in the first years of the new gospel, the cultural implications were much different for those who heard it.

An early missionary, Paul, wrote this in one of his letters, stating: "We preach Christ crucified: a stumbling block to Jews and foolishness to Gentiles" (1 Corinthians 1:23 NIV).

The stumbling block to the Jews resulted from their preconceptions of their Messiah. The Jews had been waiting centuries for him, believing he would rescue them from their Roman oppressors. How could they believe this man from Nazareth was the Messiah?

He had been born to a poor, young, unknown woman among cattle and donkeys. He relied on charity as he taught. He belonged to no school of religious establishment. And—the stumbling block mentioned by Paul—he had been crucified.

Only criminals were crucified. Only a man without power would allow himself to be slaughtered publicly. This was their long-promised, all-powerful Messiah?

As for those outside the Jewish heritage—the Greeks and Romans who were among the first Gentiles to hear the gospel— this crucifixion was an even greater stumbling block to accepting Jesus. For they were asked to put faith in a man who, as Luke reported, sweated the blood of fear in the garden of Gethsemane (Luke 22:44), then without protest lost a civil trial to the Romans, and finally died nearly naked in front of a jeering crowd.

The religious legends of the Greeks and Romans were peopled by gods of great beauty and nobility. For the proud men and women who worshipped those gods, there was nothing heroic or manly about Jesus—or his disciples—in the last days before the crucifixion.

What was there for Romans and Greeks to respect? Judas was a traitor. Peter denied his teacher to avert his own arrest. The other disciples didn't fight to protect Jesus. In his prayer in the garden of Gethsemane, Jesus himself pleaded with God for anything but the crucifixion. On the day of his death, Jesus didn't even have the strength to carry his cross; a stranger was forced to do it for him. And finally, unlike what usually happened in the dramatic Greek and Roman legends, death simply arrived for Jesus, with no dramatic rescue or escape.

The crucifixion and the brutal honesty of the Gospel writers worked against them as they tried to spread the message. The writers showed themselves and their misunderstandings of Jesus and his kingdom teachings. The writers described their doubts, shame, cowardice, and failings. They never flinched from telling it the way it was.

Yes, for Jews and Gentiles there was nothing glorious about a man on a cross. Indeed, the crucifixion—and all that led to it—was a stumbling block to the Jews and foolishness to the Gentiles.

Yet in weakness there is truth.

Listeners to the gospel in Paul's time would never mistake the story for embellished legend. In the same way, readers today can be assured that after twenty centuries, the reality of the stories have lost none of the freshness they held when Matthew, Mark, Luke, and John and the other disciples were actually witnessing to others in the market, on the road, and in front of crowds.

How important is this truth?

It is on the resurrection of Jesus that everything else about him rests.

But can you believe something this unthinkable actually happened?

Can you believe something as unthinkable as the resurrection actually happened?

Remember the reaction to Jesus' healings and miracles. Lazarus is raised from the dead and the religious authorities mutter, "What are we going to do?…This man certainly performs many miraculous signs. If we leave him alone, the whole nation will follow him, and then the Roman army will come and destroy both our Temple and our nation" (John 11:47,48).

Thus, even Jesus' opponents confirm his miracles. Yes, it could be argued that the Gospel writer decided to put these words into the mouths of the authorities to make fictionalized accounts of miracles more real. But the fact remains, the authorities saw no choice but to kill Jesus, and no historian, believer or not, argues the truth of the crucifixion.

In other words, something extraordinary about Jesus was responsible for how the world reacted to him. If the stories of the miracles were added later to the Gospels as some might argue, why the crucifixion, the hatred, and hostility of the religious and political authorities?

To accept the resurrection, you must first accept the miracles and healings.

Some deny it all, saying that miracles and healings contradict fixed laws of nature.

Yet how fixed are these laws? And even if fixed, how well do we truly understand them?

The universe is an incredible, awesome place with mysteries beyond our grasp. In this universe, where even scientists admit the unfathomable, is it difficult to accept the possibility of miracles? If Jesus was who he claimed to be, can we accept that there is much we will never comprehend about how he did what he did?

Rationalists say there is an explanation for everything. They cling to this belief like survivors of a shipwreck cower inside a lifeboat, afraid to look over the edge at the immense ocean on which they float. But what about the mystery of love? What about human passion and inspiration that is reflected in music, art, poetry, and novels?

When we say that a miracle is a suspension of the laws of nature or an exception to the laws of nature, we also say that reality is a fixed and closed system. Can any human say this with authority? Instead, should we not consider miracles as an elevation of nature, reminding us that reality is not fixed and closed, but is wonderfully open and filled with mysterious possibilities by an equally incomprehensible God?

Approaching the Gospels with this understanding, then, allows for the miracles of Jesus to take place within the realm of this universe. It also takes us beyond the cross with the fearful hope and trust that his disciples experienced when they found the empty tomb.

Here is what the Gospels report:

Jesus died on the cross. His side was pierced by a sword; had he been alive, the soldiers would have broken his legs to hasten his death by suffocation, as reported in John 19:33. His body was placed in a tomb belonging to a rich man named Joseph of Arimathea. At the request of the religious authorities, this tomb was guarded by Roman soldiers. A large rock, which took several men to roll, was placed in front of the entrance. On Sunday morning, the tomb was found empty, the rock rolled away, with the soldiers long scattered. (Both the friends of Jesus and his enemies agreed that the tomb was empty and that the corpse was never found.) After that, Jesus appeared to his friends and disciples. Since then, no one has been able to prove the resurrection occurred.

Just as importantly, however, no one has been able to prove it did *not* occur.

Nobody has ever been able to prove the resurrection did *not* occur.

The details of his crucifixion match historical records of the process, including the note in John about soldiers breaking the legs of criminals on either side of him to hasten their deaths. To suggest that Jesus didn't die on the cross but went into a brief coma and revived in the coolness of the tomb is hardly plausible. And if it did happen, and he woke trapped inside, who rolled the massive stone away for him?

Certainly not Jesus. If he was simply a man, revived from a coma, where would he get the strength?

Certainly not the Roman soldiers, who faced possible execution for failing in their duty.

Certainly not his enemies, who wanted the tomb guarded. (If you want to argue that they changed their minds and stole the corpse to prevent the rise of a Jesus cult, why would they not produce the body later when his resurrection was proclaimed?)

And certainly not his unarmed disciples, so afraid of the Romans that they did not even take part in the burial of their master. If they had arrived to move away the stone, how? These were peasants, unskilled at fighting. Nor would they have been able to sneak in and move something that massive away—even sleeping soldiers would surely have been alerted by their efforts.

Those who argue that the disciples stole the body of Jesus fail to find an explanation for how an unarmed band of fishermen and tradesmen overpowered the Roman soldiers who guarded the tomb and removed the body unnoticed.

Why would they have stolen his body in the first place? To invent a story of a resurrected Jesus would ensure that they would gain little except their own deaths. Persecution by the Jewish and Roman authorities would follow.

Also, there was no way the disciples could forecast the importance of a risen Jesus as the cornerstone of a new faith. His followers could have compiled his teachings and passed them on, avoiding risk of ridicule and persecution by insisting Jesus had risen from the dead.

Without the astonishing truth of a risen Jesus, it is difficult to explain the incredible transformation in a pitiful group of cowards that pushed them to endure whippings, beatings, prison, and martyrdom on his behalf. The historically unique explosion of new Christian communities in the short period after Jesus' death and the enduring faith of millions of people in the ensuing centuries make Jesus' resurrection unlikely to be a hoax or conspiracy.

As any police officer would tell you, false alibis shift and break down under interrogation. Only men and women speaking the truth would consistently stick with their stories under the pressure of persecution.

Note too, the four Gospel versions of the appearance of Jesus. Each tells a different aspect of the events immediately following the discovery of the empty tomb. All four however, show that women are the main witnesses. According to Jewish principles of evidence, the witness given by women is illegal and inadmissible. If the disciples were to make up the story of the resurrection, surely they would have used more credible witnesses. Again, the appearance of Jesus provides the best explanation for this—these women are noted in the accounts because that is exactly what happened.

Despite all these points, no amount of logical argument will prove to any one that Jesus appeared to the disciples again as reported in the Gospels.

However, logic, historical data, and consistency do point to one certain thing: While some will deny the resurrection of Jesus by clinging to the rational fact of its uniqueness in human history, neither is it irrational and foolish to accept the resurrection.

And, once accepted, there will be an overwhelming shift in your view of the world, the universe, and eternity.

TRUTH IS OUT THERE

The
MEANING

Once you accept the resurrection, there will be an overwhelming shift in your view of the world, the universe, and eternity.

Because then you understand that in this life, you are a fledgling, your soul held to the nest by the pull of gravity, time, and the spatial existence of a human body.

You understand that the God of love, who created all things we perceive as natural, stands outside of his creation in a way we can never comprehend, for he stands outside of gravity and time and spatial existence.

You understand because of his love, he is intent on opening our wings for a flight beyond the nest, a flight we cannot imagine beyond our minute span of years on a tiny planet lost in the mysteries of the universe.

If you accept that you have a soul created by the God of love, then you understand that body and soul are fused in the beginning, to be torn apart at the end. This separation is a mystery so unknowable that your every instinct and every breath will fight against the moment of death. The end of this life will be like the beginning. As a baby in the comfort of your mother's womb, the world of harsh cold air outside was a shock and the beginning of a journey you wailed against, wanting only to remain curled into a fetal ball with your mother's heartbeat the center point of your existence. So, too, for the soul as it reluctantly leaves the only world it knows, a damaged and decaying body.

If you accept you have a soul created by the God of love, then you understand that during your life on earth, your intent self-interest and self-absorption will obscure your awareness of the One who created you. Futilely searching for your own satisfaction and your own gods is a chasm between you and God that you will never cross without his help.

Reaching God requires the same elements of reaching any chosen destination, you must first know of it, then make a choice to get there, and finally, find the means to reach it. To reach God, you must first know of him, then make a choice to want to reach him, and finally find the means to cross that chasm.

If you accept you have a soul created by the God of love, you understand through Jesus that the bridge is already there, over the chasm—if you trust Jesus and his message. For when Jesus walked this earth, he was confident that God loved you without conditions or limits. He was equally confident that God's love was a gift to you. All he asks is that you accept the gift, for like any gift, it is not yours until you reach for it and take it.

That Jesus was able to shape the events in this world with power from beyond it is a strong testimony to his origin, and an equally strong testimony to the destiny which awaits you.

Still, it is not the actual sight of God on earth—through the witnesses of the Gospels—that will end your doubts and fears about the journey beyond this life. Not all who saw Jesus believed. Not all who now hear of Jesus believe.

The handicap is that you are able to view this world with only the five senses of your human body. You rely so totally on those senses, you want to believe there is nothing beyond what those senses can comprehend.

So it is faith that will give you the spiritual vision to see through the eyes of your eternal soul. And it is faith that allows the presence of God to illuminate your soul where it now resides in the prison of your body.

Faith is nothing more than trusting Jesus and his message, trusting that he proved this love by allowing Pontius Pilate to send him to the cross, trusting that he reappeared on earth after his death by some means you will not understand until your own soul leaves your body.

Can you let go and believe?

And if you do, what does accepting the resurrection of Jesus mean for your life?

What does accepting the resurrection of Jesus mean for your life?

First what it does not mean:

It does not mean you need to declare that you have reached the state of "being Christian." This phrase, unfortunately, often seems negative to those outside the circle of followers of Jesus.

While the media is often to blame for unflattering portrayals of prominent Christians or the Christian movement, those in organized Christianity must sometimes also accept responsibility.

It is unfair for Christians—as individuals or organizations—to gather in groups of self-love and self-praise and hold those outside the church to Christian standards, condemning those "sinners" accordingly. Jesus was stern about this. By his example, his followers must strive to love those outside of the church, praying and encouraging them to accept God's love while expecting the higher standards from those inside the church.

It can also be too easily argued that "Christians" publicly define themselves by who they are and what they oppose.

Jesus taught differently, directing his followers to positive acts. Listen to him in Mark 12: 30,31: "'Love the Lord your God with all your heart, all your soul, all your mind, and all your strength.' The second is equally important: 'Love your neighbor as yourself.' No other commandment is greater than these."

By example, too, Jesus became known for what he stood for. For healing, even on a Sabbath. For forgiveness not of the sin, but of the sinner. For reaching out to those in need.

In direct contrast to Jesus, the Pharisees had clearly defined what they stood against. Over generations, they had derived a legalistic structure of religion based on the Ten Commandments and the teachings of Moses. They were against travel on the Sabbath, they were against impurity, they were against women in the inner court of the temple, and on and on. In their self-righteousness, they were against the people who failed to follow their religious rules.

In this way, people or groups today are no different from the Pharisees of Jesus' time when they use the term "Christian" to justify their legalistic judgment of others, and when they are not only exclusive but unloving of those they exclude. These are the people who use anti-Jesus principles to affirm their moral superiority and scorn others who they think are not Christian.

Nor does accepting the resurrection of Jesus mean you believe in the church or a church. Instead, you believe in a God of love proclaimed by the church and its traditions, and you believe that God sent Jesus to reach you with his love.

Nor does it mean you must get embroiled in the theological debates you will be sure to encounter. Jerry B. Jenkins, cowriter of the Left Behind series, puts it this way: "The older I get, the simpler becomes my theology. I used to be able to stay up all night arguing doctrinal differences and denominational distinctives. But you quit drawing lines in the sand when you realize how few of us are left on the beach. I'm down to: God loves you, Jesus died for you, Jesus is alive, Jesus is coming again."

Accepting the resurrection simply means that you have purpose and peace and hope, which nothing else on earth can provide for your soul.

W hen you accept the resurrection, it simply means that you have purpose, peace, and hope, which nothing else on earth can provide for your soul.

This purpose, peace, and hope will add immeasurably to the rest of your life on earth.

The purpose comes from knowing that you have a destination at the end of this life's journey. Your eternal existence, then, is of great significance. To you. To God.

Because of this, every decision you face in every aspect of life matters. Will your choice lead you toward your destination? Or away?

Decisions which may seem important on the surface will mean little. Strive daily for a bigger house, a better car, more money? Do these things lead you to God? Will they matter over the course of an eternal journey?

Decisions which may seem to matter little on the surface will mean much. These are the accumulation of small daily moral choices which either contribute to strengthening or eroding your soul. How will you react to a coworker whose social skills make him the butt of jokes? With compassion? Disdain? Will you publicly admit a mistake and grow from it? Or will you choose the safety of a lie to protect your image? In the slow but certain manner that repeated footsteps across grass eventually form a path, so will each new choice contribute to forming who you become, in this life and the next.

The fact that God awaits makes it utterly compelling that you make your decisions with purpose.

Part of your purpose once you accept Jesus means living this life with the vital knowledge that God loves you. Allowing God to love you, and in turn striving to love him, will infuse all your relationships with vitality. Jesus serves as the role model for this. In the stories which bear witness of him we see that he acted with great purpose, for he knew all his actions and choices reflected God's love, whether he met someone once or spent years with them.

Peace?

If an eternal God of love is behind everything, you can let go of the futile urge to shape and control and worry. Jesus knew this well, telling his followers that no amount of worrying could add a single day to their lives. Understand that God loves you, and that he is taking care of you, even if at the moment you cannot understand where the events of this life lead you or why you face any given hardships.

For without God, your life is like a flight where you are the lone pilot in a cockpit with controls that bewilder you and an aircraft that does not respond. At the best of times, flying is difficult. During storms it is a nightmare.

For without God, even when things are going well in this life, you have emptiness in your soul. You cannot escape the crucial truth that if you feel unfilled when there are not problems, how much worse will you feel when problems arrive. And when the storms of problems arrive, as they do in all lives, without the peace of knowing God is in control, you have no foundation to give you strength to endure them.

(With God in your life, however, you do not go back to the passenger section and mutely disembark when the plane lands. No, with God in your life, you have an unseen copilot who allows you to make the flying decisions. You understand the controls of the airplane that is your life, because he has given you Jesus, who shows you how to live life with meaning. Storms do not frighten you, because your experienced copilot will not abandon you, no matter how dark the clouds or how rough the turbulence.)

And, finally, hope comes from knowing that death is not final. You need not be terrified of death. Death cannot take away your existence. It cannot take away the love you build in this world. Death cannot take away the meaning of life. Death is merely the next step in your eternal journey, and all the pain you endure in this life will be forgotten in your new life.

Can you trust Jesus, his teachings, and his resurrection to accept what will give you purpose, peace, and hope?

Because that is all it takes. Trusting Jesus.

That's all it takes. Trusting Jesus.

For some, arriving at this love is fast, intense, and certain. Like stepping from a dark cave into full sunlight.

For others, it is a slow, gradual comprehension. Like watching the sun rise over the horizon to spill its rays across the land.

Yet for others, it is a complicated dance filled with clumsy mistakes. Like standing beneath patches of dark clouds that sweep across the sky, lit occasionally by glimpses of the sun until finally the storm passes.

Every person has their own unique journey to the sun.

For me, it wasn't until I stood in the weeping chamber of his tomb, in Jerusalem, that I finally began to truly understand what the life of Jesus meant.

Until that quiet moment in a small cave carved into a hillside of stone, I had been held prisoner by those sentimental paintings of a haloed, bearded man tenderly holding a lamb; by those crayon-colored Sunday school drawings of fishermen in small wooden boats; by those sentimental Christmas carols; by those long and boring sermons on damnation or guilt or tithing properly. In short, the wall separating me from Jesus the man was built by a middle-class Protestant childhood on the eve of the third millennium in the wealthiest region of the world.

Differences?

He was a celibate Jew in a dusty, backwater province that struggled under Roman rule two thousand years ago. As for me, married less than a year, a son of Dutch immigrant parents, I was intent on writing a novel that spanned only eight days, the week of the crucifixion of this carpenter who changed the world.

How could I place myself in the life of someone who walked beside Jesus during the week of his crucifixion? How could this man Jesus and I reach across time to each other?

I knew, however, I could at least share geography with this man. So, with my wife, Cindy, I had flown to Israel, on an airplane that traveled at three-quarters of the speed of sound, some six miles above the earth. Definitely not a borrowed plodding donkey colt. What a surprise; the curtains of time did not even ripple for me.

Days passed. A blur of historic sites. The pastoral beauty of the Sea of Galilee, the hills above Capernaum, the river Jordan, Nazareth.

I did not find the gap closing between me and this man. As I walked through Israel, I held hands with someone who anchored me to love. Where Jesus, alone even among disciples who failed to understand him, defied centuries of rigid legalism in a growing showdown that would doom him to hours of agony and humiliation of public torture on a darkened Friday afternoon.

As I walked through Israel, I took what pictures I could with a disposable camera. In the same places where Jesus had been giving what he could to the wounded in spirit and flesh, bringing his radical message that we are all children of a God of love.

Still no connection, no opening of the curtain of time. Of course not.

No connection until my last day in Israel, when I stood in the weeping chamber of his tomb, overlooking the hollowed rock where it is said Joseph of Arimathea placed Jesus' body.

Near this garden is a hill that looks eerily like a skull. Golgotha. It was not named, as many think, for skulls of the dead abandoned around the execution sites; Jewish law forbade exposure of human bones. Instead, as anyone can see even today, the hill is a high, rounded rocky plateau like the dome of a man's head, worn by wind and rain to a dull gray. Two shallow caves side by side, and a lower, larger cave centered below, form the two eyes and gaping mouth of a skull. At certain times of the day, when the sun's light casts black shadows across these depressions, it creates a vision of a gaunt face. You can almost hear an ancient wind moan across its barren stone, speaking of the cries and groans and cursing of all the men who died tortured deaths within sight of these dead, dark eyes.

It was in this tomb I stood, along with others in a small group with our guide. Behind us, the mouth of the tomb was open to the sky and sunlight beyond. It was still cool, despite the day's heat, with the silence that is peculiar to any resting place for the dead.

Our guide broke this hush to quietly explain that a man of means in the time of Jesus would purchase a rocky hillside for a family tomb, and hire stone workers to carve a narrow arched entrance the height of a man's head. Through this entrance, the workers would continue to hew into the heart of the hill, widening and clearing a space inside barely higher than a man can reach and no more than seven steps in length or width.

Once the tomb had been completely hollowed, the workers then measured each grown member of the family, and chiseled graves side by side to accommodate each of their bodies upon their deaths. Graves for the children in the family would be left rough and unfinished until they were fully grown, so that the size of their graves could be accurately determined and cut only once.

When the guide told us we were standing in the weeping chamber of the tomb—a small area overlooking the graves—I had my first inkling of the shiver of understanding that would overcome me.

The weeping chamber. Where mourners washed and anointed the body with oil and perfumes, wrapped it in grave clothes made of long strips of linen, packed the linens with fragrant spices to take away the smell of death, and bound the body's head with a linen napkin.

The weeping chamber. In that moment, time's curtain first moved for me. The crucifixion began to become real to me, two thousand years later.

Then the guide pointed out the grave to our far left, the place of honor, where the head of the family would be buried. He asked us to notice that the end of that grave have been crudely hollowed out an extra few inches—as if workers had first designed it for the owner of the tomb, then hastily changed it at the last minute to accommodate a taller body.

The guide allowed us our silence of comprehension. *Joseph of Arimathea had made his last-minute decision to place Jesus' body in his own grave. And Jesus was a taller man. So they had chipped at the presized grave to make room for Jesus.*

The curtains of time opened wider for me. Yes. Jesus was a man who had walked this earth. Just like me, a fragile package of protein wrapped around hopes and fears and love. And a soul.

At that moment, my growing shiver was not a result of the cool air of the tomb.

Our guide reminded us of a verse in the Gospel of John, one that had never made sense to me until then. During Jesus' time, there was one way that a carpenter let the contractor know a job was finished. A signature, so to speak, by illiterate workers who could not leave behind notes or invoices upon completion of a job.

Instead, they left a folded cloth—the cloth they used to dry themselves after washing at the completion of the job.

As our guide spoke, I was able to imagine a hot afternoon in Galilee. Jesus at the end of a carpentry job, the hair of his strong forearms matted with sawdust and sweat. At the site of his work, he pours water over his face and chest, splashing it over his arms to clean himself before he begins his journey home. He pats his face and arms and hands dry with a towel. Jesus folds the towel neatly in half, and folds it in half again. He places it on his work and walks away.

Later, the guide explained, whoever arrived for inspection would see the towel and understand its simple message. *The work is finished.*

His disciples, of course, knew of this craftsman's tradition.

On the Sunday of sorrow that followed his death on the cross, years after Jesus had set aside his carpenter tools, Peter crouched to look into an empty tomb and saw only the linens that the risen Jesus had left behind. Peter saw the wrap which had been used to cover Jesus' face. It had been folded in half, and then folded in half once again, and was placed neatly on the stone floor of the tomb.[5]

Peter's friend, the carpenter, had left behind a simple message. *It is finished.*

It was there, in that moment in the weeping chamber of his tomb, that Jesus reached across time for me. There, that I finally began to truly understand how Jesus was man. And how Jesus was so much more than man.

Because his message had been left for me too.

STORIES
for
REFLECTION

The first of the following stories, "At the Village Gate," was written to show the society that Jesus was raised in and the religious attitudes he overcame with the message of love and forgiveness.

The second, "I Will Be Free," was written to explore what it means to have a soul.

An Introduction to "At the Village Gate"

In his classic book, *Walden*, Henry David Thoreau writes that "The mass of men lead lives of quiet desperation." This quote is famous because this sense of quiet desperation is so universal.

Most of us do live quietly, seemingly insignificant in the shadows of the spotlights cast by those who are famously rich or famously criminal or famously skilled in acting or sports or politics.

Yet it is love which makes every quiet life significant, for those who live a life of quiet desperation live without love. And in these terms, even the famous who live without love will face lives of quiet desperation.

For without love, you may speak any language—as the apostle Paul writes in 1 Corinthians 13—but your voice will be a meaningless noise like a clanging symbol. Without love, you may know all the mysteries of the future, you may have enough faith to move a mountain, you may give everything to the poor and even sacrifice your body, but you will have no value.

With love, your life will be complete. Paul writes later in that chapter that love is patient, kind, rejoices in truth, never gives up, never loses faith, is always hopeful, and endures through all circumstances.

The life of Jesus proves this.

His love was a quiet revolution, changing western civilization in a way that no other force was able. Through love, it is possible to live in a revolutionary way, even when you live quietly.

Because love cannot be defeated.

At the Village Gate

The woman's death had been decided.

And this day was the day of her death, something the children of the village sensed without quite comprehending, soaking in the excited and anticipated horror from the whispered gossip of adults.

So the children followed.

They followed behind the villagers. The villagers, in turn, followed the elders in their dusty knee-length tunics, who wore silent grimness like cloaks, their bearded faces straining with the seriousness of their task. All of them followed the woman, who walked in front of the elders, draped in a plain brown girdled blanket, her hands bound and hanging on her belly, and her freshly-shaved head bowed. The woman, the elders, the villagers, and the children, formed a small pitiful dusty procession in a small pitiful dusty village high in the rocky hills of a small pitiful provincial outpost of the Roman empire.

The death procession was made more grim by the merciless heat. The cloudless sky was white with the glare of sun. Dust rose like talcum powder as each step of each man's sandal flopped on the wide path that served as a road between the square plastered houses with palm-branch roofs. The walls of the buildings seemed to ripple from layers of shimmering air.

The men walked slowly and ignored the villagers and the children. Leading this entire procession was a synagogue herald, sweating heavily in his tasseled cassock. Their destination was the crumbling stone walls that formed the town gates.

Near the gates, fist-sized jagged rocks were piled like a cairn.

At every few steps, the herald called out a singsong proclamation of ritual, as if he served an audience of hundreds instead of only the population of a tiny, obscure village. As required by law, the herald called out the same proclamation one final time as all of them neared the gates.

"Jaala Mehetabel, wife of Lachish, the son of Sabian of Beth She'arim, is going forth to be stoned because she has dishonored him and his name through the act of adultery. Nadabb, son of Nodab, and Seth of Kedesh are witnesses against her. If anyone knows anything in favor of her acquittal, let him come forth and plead it."

No one came forth. The evidence was irrefutable. Late one evening an unidentified and still unknown man had been seen entering her house. This man was not her husband, for Lachish son of Sabian had been in nearby Japhia for a week-long feast to celebrate a nephew's wedding. The witnesses that night were impeccable and beyond refute: Nadabb and Seth were two of the town's elders. They had immediately undertaken a vigil outside of the house, determined to identify this intruder. Unfortunately for their curiosity, the seated old men had fallen asleep, each against the other, during their wait to identify the man on his departure.

Within an hour of the sunrise that followed, all the adults in this small village had shared and reshared those scant details through endless gossip. Jaala Mehetabel, wife of Lachish, the son of Sabian of Beth She'arim, had not called out for help, some said, so obviously the intruder had been a welcome guest. Others laughed, saying the man must have been dragged in by rope, for Jaala was no woman of beauty. All agreed, however, it was a shame that the town elders had fallen asleep, for according to law, both the man and the adulterous woman must die.

The subsequent trial had been swift, the judgment rendered as commanded by rabbinic law, the rocks readied. So now the herald, and the procession that followed him, continued in the midday heat toward the town gates.

Ten cubits from the place of execution, the herald stopped. So did the entire procession, with the children straining to peer around the larger bodies of the adults. The herald turned to face the woman with the shaved head.

"Make your confession," he commanded her, for ancient law required the statement at exactly this distance from the town gates.

Jaala Mehetabel, wife of Lachish, the son of Sabian of Beth She'arim, raised her head and stared the herald directly in the eyes. She had a square face, the flesh just starting to sag with age. Her eyebrows were thick and dull brown, the same color her thin hair had been before the men had held her down and sheared her indifferently as they would a sheep to be readied for slaughter. Her lips, like her chunky body, had no curves. She had folded her bound hands together, and the skin showed work scars on red, swollen knuckles. Any beauty she had was in her eyes, which glowed from a mixture of fear and defiance, and strangely, joy.

"Make your confession," the herald demanded again. Everyone expected her to make the ritualistic reply as the occasion demanded. *May my death be an atonement for all my sins.* This would cleanse her of evil, this would cleanse the land of evil.

Her answer instead was continued silence.

"Make your confession," the herald commanded once again, his tone higher with restrained anger.

She did not.

The herald looked to the town elders for guidance.

"Let her die without peace then," a man said at the front of the crowd. He was the largest of them, with the face above his untrimmed beard permanently flushed red from the years of food and wine that had also given him his bulk.

"As you say," the herald said. After all, aside from Moses, who was a greater authority on her punishment than this man, Lachish son of Sabian, her husband and also her formal accuser?

Lachish waved the men behind him to move forward and push the woman toward the stone wall. They grabbed her arms to force her forward. She shook them off and walked alone to her place of execution.

She faced them, her large hands clenched and straining at the bounds of rope. Defiance finally lost to fear. Tears as thick as blood welled in the corners of her eyes.

Even now, the elders were not ready to take rocks from the nearby pile. Two marched to the woman. Wordlessly, without resistance from her, they stripped the brown tunic from her body and left it at her feet. Because of the watching children, they allowed her undergarments to remain in place. This limited exposure, however, showed the entire village that her body held little attraction for any man. This renewed humiliation brought her head down once more.

The two elders returned to the group.

Lachish, son of Sabian, was the first man to step to the pile of rocks. As accuser, he would be the first to throw.

The other men followed and armed themselves with jagged rocks.

In this moment, a sudden gust of wind broke the heat's stranglehold, coming up from the valley and kicking dust. Somewhere from the crowd, a woman wailed. The men of the procession closed their mouths tighter and squinted their eyes against the swirling dust. Neither wind nor mourning would stop them from their duty.

They all waited for Lachish, her husband. The stoning could not begin until he cast the first stone. He hefted the rock in his right hand.

Jaala Mehetabel, wife of Lachish, the son of Sabian of Beth She'arim, raised her head again.

"No," she cried above the rising wind. "Not until I speak."

The men hesitated.

With both bound hands, she raised her arms and pointed at her husband Lachish. "I was sold to this man by my father, a man who drank too much wine and beat me when it suited him. My husband saw fit to continue my father's habit."

"Enough woman!" Lachish roared. "You have no say."

She ignored him and directed her words to all the town elders. "I have been nothing more to him than a beast, an animal to work his fields and household. I have seen this man pat a mule's neck and comfort the beast with more kindness than he has ever shown me. This is a man who inflicted upon his wife public shame by leaving her behind when he attended a wedding no farther away than a half hour's travel."

The women in the crowd muttered agreement. Many shared her sentiments toward their own husbands and wanted to applaud her anger. But she would be dead soon, and they would have to continue to live with the men who treated them no better than mules.

At the muttering, Lachish raised his hand to throw a rock. The elder beside him restrained his arm.

"It must not be thrown in anger," the elder said to Lachish. "We punish her in duty."

"She has brought death upon herself," Lachish snarled. "It is the law."

"Listen to me," the woman cried. "You know how much dishonor there is for a woman to be sent away by her man.

Even so, I would have begged him to release me and I would have gladly fled. Yet I had no place to go, no family to take me. So I was forced to stay.

"Listen to me. The women of this village shunned me, and I visited the well alone. Unlike even cows or sheep, I could find no comfort with others like me."

The wind swirled at her feet, pulling at the hem of her undergarments.

"Not once in my life had the warmth of any love touched me," she cried. "Until another man saw beyond this wretched, worn appearance. And I was loved."

Now the tears rolled freely down her plain face.

"Loved," she said. "Loved in spirit, not in body. Loved and respected so much that not once did this man touch me. He gave me a far greater gift. He spoke to me and gave me comfort through the long, lonely hours."

She wiped her face awkwardly with her bound hands, smearing her dusty tear-streaked cheeks.

"If accepting love and comfort from another when my own husband treated me as an animal is a sin, then I confess it freely in front of God and his people. If spending cold lonely nights in the company of a man who loved me but did not touch me in an adulterous way is a sin, then I confess it freely in front of God and his people. If death is the price I pay for that comfort and love, I gladly accept it for the short time that love touched my barren life."

Her lips began to quiver as she fought for more words, fought for new courage. She drew breath and said with a quietness barely heard above the storm, "Stone me if you will."

"Moses has commanded us to purge this evil from the people," Lachish shouted. He wrenched his arm from the man beside him, and hurled a rock at his wife.

It struck her in the upper arm, gashing a streak of bright red.

"You want to know who he was," she taunted her husband. "It drives you mad with anger to think any other man might take a possession of yours. In my death, I take satisfaction in knowing you aren't able to kill him alongside me."

Lachish transferred the other rock from his left hand to his right, and threw it in full rage. She chose not to duck, and it hit her cheekbone, knocking her to her knees.

"I will not tell you who he is," she said, her words difficult to understand through broken teeth. "You will not kill him with me."

Before any of the other town elders could throw, a man from the small crowd of villagers broke loose and ran toward her.

"No!" he cried. "No! I cannot be among those who watch!"

He was a tiny man with a crippled left arm. Thin. Dressed in rags. He fell to his knees, wrapped his right arm around the broadness of her upper body in an effort to provide her protection with his own body.

"The dung collector!" laughed Lachish, relieved it was not a man of higher stature who had somehow seen an overlooked value in his wife. "Can you do no better?"

Neither the little man nor the big woman gave a sign that either had heard. Each clung to the other, murmuring words of love. He, the man who made a living by searching the rocky hills for dry dung to sell as fuel for cooking. She, a worn, childless woman with no friends in the village.

Lachish, son of Sabian, gave the signal. Rocks rained down on both.

The tiny man died on his knees, his arms around her, his face away from the men of the village. The woman's face, however, was clear to the men above the tiny man's shoulder, and showed a smile which remained until the final light left her eyes.

Behind the elders silently intent on throwing the rocks, behind the villagers and older children who jeered the death of the dung collector and the ugly woman, was a young boy. He was the son of Joseph and Mary, born in another village to the south because of a census decreed by the emperor Augustus and enforced by Quirinius, governor of Syria.

Few others around understood what this boy, despite his youth, understood and perhaps even foresaw for himself on that day in the small, dusty village of Nazareth. Man and law, even armed with death as the greatest and final weapon, can never defeat love.

JOHN 8:1-11
(New International Version)

Jesus went to the Mount of Olives. At dawn he appeared again in the temple courts, where all the people gathered around him, and he sat down to teach them. The teachers of the law and the Pharisees brought in a woman caught in adultery. They made her stand before the group and said to Jesus, "Teacher, this woman was caught in the act of adultery. In the Law Moses commanded us to stones such women. Now what do you say?" They were using this question as a trap, in order to have a basis for accusing him.

But Jesus bent down and started to write on the ground with his finger. When they kept on questioning him, he straightened up and said to them, "If any one of you is without sin, let him be the first to throw a stone at her." Again he stooped down and wrote on the ground.

At this, those who heard began to go away one at a time, the older ones first, until only Jesus was left, with the woman still standing there. Jesus straightened up and asked her, "Woman, where are they? Has no one condemned you?"

"No one, sir," she said.

"Then neither do I condemn you," Jesus declared. "Go now and leave your life of sin."

An Introduction to "I Will Be Free"

I confess I took inspiration and the story title—with permission—from a video and song written and performed by my wife, recording artist Cindy Morgan. The song always moves me and fills me with hope. I know I am not alone in this, for it is a song that celebrates freedom in the face of death.

Freedom.

To varying degrees, all of us are imprisoned by our bodies. Even gifted professional athletes face physical limitations dictated by the human structure of muscle and bone. They are capable of feats of skill and strength that set them apart from millions of other less gifted humans, yet they cannot soar on the wind like hawks, they cannot knife miles through water like sharks. Professional athletes, like the rest of us, are earthbound, relatively clumsy creatures. And they, like the rest of us, face the limitations of sickness, age, and death.

Freedom.

From that perspective, our physical selves matter little—from a person in a wheelchair to a mountain climber in his prime. Because death takes even the strongest, wealthiest, wisest of us, the only freedom we can find is freedom of the spirit.

Faith in that freedom of spirit takes our focus from what binds us here on earth and lifts our eyes to something much grander than our physical restrictions.

On a practical level, I believe that the same faith gives us a truer perspective of our earthbound troubles. Nothing on earth, not even death, is so overwhelming that it can take away the freedom of our spirit. And with that understanding, troubles are much easier to face.

Because humans were born to soar.

I Will Be Free

We had agreed—the woman I loved and I—that as soon as the child was born, we would perform an act of mercy and decency and wrap it in a towel to drown it in a nearby sink, like a kitten in a sack dropped into a river. But in the motel room that was our home, the woman I loved died while giving birth, and her child, a grotesque tiny bundle of strangely silent vulnerability, was all that remained to remind me of her. I was nearly blind with tears in that lonely motel room at the side of a highway, and with the selfishness typical of my entire life to that point, I delayed the mercy and decency we had promised the baby. I used the towel not to wrap and drown the little girl, but to clean her dry of blood and placenta.

In the moment as I lifted her twisted, misshapen arms and gently wiped the terrible hunch in the center of her back, where her arms connected to a ridge of bone that pushed against her translucent skin, I heard God speak to me for the first time in my life. He did not speak in the loud and terrible way as claimed by the preachers of these Appalachian mountains where I eventually sought refuge with the child. Instead God spoke in the way I believe God most often speaks to humans—through the heart, when circumstances have stripped away our obstinate self-focus. In that moment, holding this girl child in her first moments outside the womb, my revulsion gave way to protective love. In that moment, my life was transformed far more than I would have ever believed when I made a decision to turn my back on my science for the woman I loved.

That was fifteen years ago, and although I knew then that the day would arrive when I would have to pay the price for this love, it has still arrived far, far too soon...

—Papa, Katrina says to me. —Where are we going?

Our cabin is behind us. The door is locked. When the men we flee break down the door, a switch will trigger an explosion. Tear gas, not nitro. I do not wish them dead. Only delayed.

—Please trust me, I tell my Katrina. —You will find out soon enough.

She nods. She is tiny, but not elf-like. To me, the beauty in her face gives her a dignity much greater than her lack of size. I also see the trust I have requested.

I feel like Abraham, taking Isaac to the top of the mountainside. I understand the ache he must have felt as they slowly moved upward. I understand the trembling mixture of faith and hope and sadness that must have burdened him. All that is different are the mountains. His mountain was dusty, strewn with rocks and shrubs. My mountain is deep in the southern Appalachians, green with pine, alive with birds and snakes, a clear river rushing its course below. And, of course, Abraham traveled with a son. I have a daughter, not by blood, but by love.

—Will it take us long to get there? my beautiful daughter asks.

—I hope not, I say.

Which is truth. With those in pursuit, we do not have time. But my answer is also a lie. I know what waits us at the top. I wish it would take forever to get there.

It is ancient science now, human genetics. Sixty years ago, just into this new millennium, the Human Genome Project was completed. Its goal, lofty at the time, was to map out the entire genetic code of *homo sapiens*. When scientists were able to understand the purpose of every strand of human DNA, advances in medicine became astoundingly rapid. For the wealthy, embryonic screening eliminated every hereditary disease. Most couples with enough income elected test-tube fertilization, followed by implantation into the mother if the embryonic cells proved satisfactory for long-term health, eye-color, height, and other factors dictated by the parents. Insurance companies and large corporations benefited too—a single hair or fingernail clipping was enough genetic evidence to determine if its owner was a suitable risk for insurance or employment. Cloning became a hotly debated outrage in the same way that abortion on demand had once caused horrendous division. Then, like abortion, cloning became commonplace and accepted by too many in a world weary of fighting evils. The unspecialized cells of the unborn were perfect for genetic manipulation, and brain stem tissue from aborted fetuses led to a thriving organ cultivation industry. The wealthy were able to extend their lives by purchasing new hearts and livers custom ordered from a laboratory.

Then the government realized that these advances in human genetic manipulation had military potential.

—This reminds me of the picnics we have shared, Katrina says, a smile across her face.

Indeed, it is a day for a picnic. A rare day of no clouds. Little wind. At the top, where the trees have thinned and the mountain is almost bare rock, I know the wind will be stronger. I pray it will be stronger.

—I always enjoyed those, I say.

I do not tell her more. That those picnics, sitting at the edge of cliffs, overlooking the valley, were also times of sadness for me. I would wonder about the woman I loved, imagine she was with us too. My deeper sadness was in observing little Katrina as she marveled at the hawks soaring below us, flashing their shadows across the tops of the pines of the valley. Katrina watched with unknowing longing, the way, I believe, God's touch makes our human souls instinctively yearn for a place we have never been.

—Remember, Katrina says, looking behind us and down at the river, —how you would tell me that our souls will someday fly?

I am startled and half-guilty, afraid that somehow she is reading my thoughts.

—Yes, I tell my beautiful daughter. —We have all been designed to soar with angels. Our souls will someday leave the prisons of our bodies and return home.

I repeat myself.

—All of us, I tell her. —In one way or another, God allows us to fly.

At the one-cell stage, an embryo is much like an egg. The outer cell wall is like the shell. The nucleus at the center is like the yolk. This nucleus contains the microscopic strands of DNA that program the growth of that embryo. Soon the single cell divides into two cells, then four, then eight, and so on. God's incredible simplicity is at work—each new cell contains the exact copy of the DNA code of the original nucleus; different strands of DNA are programmed to become active as the cells begin to specialize. Because every cell contains the entire DNA code for that organism, any changes inserted into the nucleus at the one-cell stage will be replicated in every new cell created. Scientists learned early to take advantage of this. Even before the millennium, they created flies which had up to fourteen pairs of eyes, simply by adding a snippet of DNA at the one-cell stage. Genetic manipulation at the embryonic level is known as germ-line therapy, for once the embryo matures to adult and reproduces, through its offspring, it will pass these changes to the next generation of its species. This biotechnology, and the funds and the secret blessing of certain military agencies, literally gave scientists the power to begin to reengineer the human species.

I was one of those scientists.

—Papa, Katrina says. She points below us. —Is that smoke? Near our cabin?

—Yes.

Earlier in the day, George had stopped by. He is older than I am, but born and raised in the valley, much more spry. George told me about the strangers who had arrived and asked about a deformed girl. George told me he sent them the other direction, but knew the strangers would be back. I thanked George calmly so that he would not be afraid for us. Then I pulled together all that I had prepared for this day.

—Do you suppose our cabin is on fire?

—Perhaps, I say.

I take her hand. Her fingers are much like long claws. I have learned to love those fingers and hands.

—Come, I tell her. —We must continue to climb. What happens to the cabin no longer matters to us.

I am not a man that women look at twice. Yet she did, the woman I loved. Katrina. The name I would give to our child in honor of her memory. The woman I loved was a dark-haired beauty. She was among perhaps a dozen surrogate mothers at our institution, paid to carry implanted embryos to term. She saw beyond my lab coat, slight build, slight paunch, and slightly balding head, and saw something in my eyes perhaps, a loneliness of soul that touched her. At first, our eyes held contact longer than necessary. On my later visits, we exchanged smiles. Our first tentative conversations. A touch of fingertip to fingertip. So it grew, our love, until we pledged to seek a life beyond the institution, once her body had fulfilled its contract by delivering the baby she carried.

She was six months pregnant when I discovered there would be no life beyond for her. The secrets of the institution were too grave and troubling to be risked. It was no coincidence that females selected as surrogate mothers had no other family to initiate troublesome investigations when they did not return to the outer world. It was my decision to take her away. My decision to give up science and become a fugitive with her. I had discovered love, and through it, my soul first became aware of its own existence within me. We escaped. Became man and wife. Pledged together to be parted by nothing short of death.

Our pledge lasted until the end of her pregnancy, when death arrived to take her with a hemorrhage I could not stop in that lonely, lonely motel room, where my other Katrina was thrust into this world among the echoes of her mother's groans of death.

—I am hot, Katrina says.

It is not complaint. She never complains.

I understand it is a question. *May she remove the coat?*

Rarely do I allow it. Isolated as this valley is, men still travel through it. On other occasions in other valleys, when I was less cautious, prying eyes forced us to move. The loose coat with the long, wide sleeves is our only protection.

—Let me carry your coat.

She is surprised and grateful. Her smile tinges me with deep sorrow. I take the coat.

I know, of course, what lies beneath it. I know the thinness of her body, the ribs pressed so tight against skin, the unnatural length of her delicate legs in comparison to her upper body. Today, she wears a tight sheer fabric that does little more than allow her modesty.

We continue to walk up a trail that I have placed in my memory from a dozen trips to scout the suitability of our destination. I have a hip pack belted to my waist. That is all we carry. Aside from the coat.

It is the coat which has always restricted her freedom.

We were at a church gathering in a small town along an abandoned railroad, deep in a valley in the Appalachians. Children were playing around the adults, who stood in a tight group to discuss the weather and the sermon. Katrina had slipped loose from me, to stare curiously at the other children. There was such longing in her eyes that I did not call her back. Another girl, tiny like her, approached shyly. I let them talk, happy that Katrina was happy.

Too late, I noticed that Katrina had wandered among the boys, who were rough and tumble and pushed her to the ground. Her new friend helped her up, and patted Katrina on the back. From where I stood, much too distant to be able to prevent it, I could see the curiosity on that little girl's face as her hand bumped the hump on Katrina's back, the hump hidden by her loose coat. A question was asked, and Katrina in her innocence began to shed her coat.

I ran, shouting. I arrived soon enough to prevent other adults from seeing, but three of the nearby children glimpsed enough of her mutated arms—terribly thin and long, dark with shaggy and coarsened hair—to scream and fall back in horror. I scooped Katrina in my arms, my sorrow renewed at the lightness of her bones, and fled the crowd, knowing we would have to pack our meager possessions by nightfall, and once again outrun the rumors and move deeper into the mountains.

Katrina never made the mistake again of joining with other children. Not because I warned her against it.

But because she finally understood she was different.

—I love you, I tell Katrina.

We are three-quarters of the way to the top. There is so much I want to say.

She smiles, a smile which pierces my heart.

—I love you, Papa.

There are hawks above us, taking advantage of the updrafts and the wind that blows this far up the mountain. The hawks are half a mile up in the air, trusting in the fabric of nothingness that carries them.

—Your love is my joy, I answer.

I say nothing else, realizing I must also trust a fabric of nothingness, all the invisible things I have taught her.

Smoke drifts and spreads across the valley from our cabin.

We continue our journey, with the silence of the valley pressing upon us.

Unlike Katrina, I could not entirely endure the solitude inflicted upon us by the deep and rugged valleys of the Appalachians. On Sundays, I would lock the door and leave her in the cabin for a few hours, and go to church. I first went because it was the safest way to lose myself anonymously in a small crowd; I could listen to others and make small talk when pressed, without placing myself into an intimate conversation or friendship. I enjoyed the music. I enjoyed listening to unsophisticated preachers, and I enjoyed dissecting their sermons for errors in logic, syntax, and omission. That was my weekly entertainment.

Yet truth is a diamond; mishandled, smeared with grease or buried in mud, it cannot be marred and waits for one with a cloth to polish it again. That was how God spoke to me again. Through those preachers. I finally understood, despite the distortions applied by hellfire sermons and exhortations for collection plate money. God loved me. Once God had visited this earth to deliver that message, and he was crucified for teaching that love, and now my soul was destined to join with him. I was astounded and grateful at this realization. As a scientist, it had never been difficult to acknowledge that there was a Creator behind the universe— the marvels of DNA, the exquisite dance of electron and proton, the boggling forces of gravity and light, all of it forced many of us in science away from agnosticism. Yet to comprehend that this Creator loved us more deeply than I loved Katrina gave my life renewed meaning.

Deep in the Appalachians, I had found the most important diamond any man can find—God loved me, and forgave me, even with young Katrina as a daily reminder of how terribly I had sinned.

—Are you tired? Katrina asks.

Her long dark hair is tied behind her head, resting on the hump that others think might belong to a freak.

—No. We must keep moving.

—Why?

She asks sweetly, no hint of worry on her face. She is, as I asked, trusting me.

—Why? You will find out soon, I answer.

I do not wish her to be alarmed. I am certain the men below us are in pursuit, but she does not need to fear what I fear.

Already, the trees around us are barren and stunted, thrust to the sky at awkward angles from the massive stone of the mountaintop. We near our destination.

For years, Katrina and I were safe, simply because the greatest empire the world has ever known was as dependent on water as any primitive culture. The Great Water Wars distracted our government for almost a decade, until it emerged at the top of a coalition of developed nations which survived by literally sucking lesser developed nations dry. Once our nation's fabled economy began to hum again, the military machine went back to previous tasks, including the search for better soldiers through human genetic manipulation. My desertion of the machine was once again relevant, and the agency began its pursuit again.

I did not regret withdrawing from the civilized world. Others may have their memory bank transfers in lieu of vacations, their biological insertions of computer chips to efficiently monitor body functions. I now prefer a fire on a starlit night, the sounds of the insects like a blanket over me, Katrina curled against my chest. I did regret that even the isolated valleys could not keep me safe. The trail of rumors behind us was like a faint scent on wet grass, enough to bring the hounds of my past into the tranquility that Katrina and I shared. I only wish they would have arrived a month later. A week later. A day later. Even hours later. Katrina may now be ready. But it is only belief, not certainty.

When the top of the mountain arrives, I must test that belief.

—Is there a trail down the other side, Katrina asks.

She knows the back side of this mountain is sheer granite. Now there is worry in her voice. Worry for me. She sees that my face is hot with exertion, hears my hard breathing. She does not believe I am capable of climbing down.

—Yes.

I do not tell her that only one of us will go, that the other will remain.

Because we lived in solitude, Katrina did not have any standards of normalcy to measure her life against. When I was a scientist, someone could have explained it to me, yet it would not have stopped me, for I would have understood it only in the abstract. Now I understand differently. Regardless of the changes we make to the human body through genetic manipulation, the result will still be human. Indeed, to label the result as "result" is evil, for every creature born will have a heart and soul, despite any outward appearance.

I know this, for I have lived with and loved Katrina, when once, at the embryonic stage, beneath a microscope, she was merely a "result" to me. I believe I have been punished for my scientific arrogance. While in her innocence she is unable to comprehend what science has stolen from her, I knew, every day, what she was missing from a normal childhood. Every day, my heart was broken again at the solitude and loneliness I had inflicted upon her with that single injection of DNA strand into the single embryonic cell which became her being.

The only advantage of her innocence and solitude was that she did not think it strange, the regimen of exercises she endured every day without complaint. With little available for equipment, I rigged bags of sand she pulled toward herself by rope and pulley; she did hundreds of push-ups, hundreds of chin pulls. The exercise which puzzled her most was the half-hour a day I asked her to hang in the shape of a cross, feet down, head high, arms extended with wrist, elbow and shoulder joints locked. I pushed her to exhaustion, amazed at the strength, size, and lightness of the incredibly tough muscle fibers of her shoulders and chest and upper arms.

Her growth left me both ashamed and proud of what I had accomplished as a scientist.

—Where is the trail, Papa? The trail to take us down the other side?

We are at the pinnacle of the mountain. The trail we climbed is a snake leading back to our cabin. Down the other side, the drop into the neighboring valley dizzies me. This ancient rift of stone is a chasm a half mile wide. Far, far below sunlight bounces off a curve of river.

—Papa?

I realize I haven't answered her. Up here, wind pulls at the loose ends of Katrina's hair. My eyes lift from the shine of the river and I direct my focus to meet her eyes with mine.

I still do not answer.

There is a shift in the muscles of her face. This is the moment she realizes our journey is different than all the other times we have fled.

—I love you, I say again.

In the last few months, other changes rapidly inflicted themselves on Katrina's body, triggered by her first menstrual cycle. She became voraciously hungry, especially for milk and meats. The coarse hair that draped her shoulders and upper back and arms became thicker than straw, shiny and swelling until near bursting, until the outer layers of what had once been hair became dull with a sheath of dead, flaky skin. Her fear with her first menstrual cycle I was able to explain. Her arms, I could do little except assure her that it was what her body was meant to be.

I did not care to explain that as the scientist who had viewed her first moments of life under a microscope, I knew what the DNA snippet I had added was programmed to do. A truth untold is also a lie; I justified it by telling myself she would discover the purpose for herself when her body was ready. I also told myself that the surprise and joy of that discovery would be worth the fear of her uncertainty.

If only I could share that joy with her.

—Turn around, I tell my beautiful daughter.

She hesitates.

—Turn around. Spread your arms.

She hears the near anger in my voice. She does as I command.

I take my hip pack off my waist. Secure it around hers.

—In here is everything you need.

Inside the hip pack is a lightweight cloak of space age material, folded to the size of a packet of tissues. It will cover her and hide her deformity. There is money. And a letter explaining the remainder of what she needs to know.

—Papa?

I strip the dead skin off her arms, peeling it away as I would the dead skin off a snake. Beneath the dead skin, it is lustrous and shiny.

—Hush, my beautiful child.

I continue to pull off the skin, satisfied at the ease with which it is removed. Yes, her body is ready.

—Papa?

Her voice holds fear. The wind is pushing at her outspread arms. She tries to fold her arms together so that the wind will pass by her instead of lifting her off her feet.

—No, I say. I push her arms apart again. —You were born for this.

—Papa?

I walk around her. She sees the tears in my eyes.

—Papa?

She is beautiful. It is not the beauty that any other father will see in his daughter. But truly beautiful.

Her outstretched arms, hinged on the hump of her back, are no longer the arms of a freak. Her coarse hair has been transformed. Her thin light bones are no longer a fragile curse.

She stands before me with her wings shiny and new.

—Fly, I tell my beautiful daughter. —You were born to fly.

—What will you do, Papa?

—I will watch, I say.

I glance over my shoulder. Those who pursue us are near.

—Fly, I say.

She trembles. An instinct in her has been awakened.

I know that once the draft takes her, she will not be able to return to this pinnacle. Later, perhaps, after she has mastered her wings. But not now.

—You must go, I say.

I smile, sadly. —There are others like you. Find them.

—Papa?

I have pushed her. As a father first releases the bicycle seat to let his child ride unassisted.

Katrina falls forward into the abyss. Without thought, she reacts to the wind. The subtle adjustments of her wings are instinctive.

The wind takes her away and she soars into the abyss. She is free.

I hear from her a cry of joy. A gift from her to me.

She becomes a distant speck, lost against the shine of the river below.

I will wait for my pursuers to reach me. They will kill me, I am sure. This location is too convenient. They will kill me, and hurl my body into the abyss.

And then, I too, will be free.

The Gospel of Mark

(New International Version)

John the Baptist Prepares the Way

1 The beginning of the gospel about Jesus Christ, the Son of God.

[2]It is written in Isaiah the prophet:

"I will send my messenger ahead of you,
 who will prepare your way"—
[3]"a voice of one calling in the desert,
'Prepare the way for the Lord,
make straight paths for him.'"

[4]And so John came, baptizing in the desert region and preaching a baptism of repentance for the forgiveness of sins. [5]The whole Judean countryside and all the people of Jerusalem went out to him. Confessing their sins, they were baptized by him in the Jordan River. [6]John wore clothing made of camel's hair, with a leather belt around his waist, and he ate locusts and wild honey. [7]And this was his message: "After me will come one more powerful than I, the thongs of whose sandals I am not worthy to stoop down and untie. [8]I baptize you with water, but he will baptize you with the Holy Spirit."

The Baptism and Temptation of Jesus

[9]At that time Jesus came from Nazareth in Galilee and was baptized by John in the Jordan. [10]As Jesus was coming up out of the water, he saw heaven being torn open and the Spirit descending on him like a dove. [11]And a voice came from heaven: "You are my Son, whom I love; with you I am well pleased."

[12]At once the Spirit sent him out into the desert, [13]and he was in the desert forty days, being tempted by Satan. He was with the wild animals, and angels attended him.

The Calling of the First Disciples

[14]After John was put in prison, Jesus went into Galilee, proclaiming the good news of God. [15]"The time has come," he said. "The kingdom of God is near. Repent and believe the good news!"

[16]As Jesus walked beside the Sea of Galilee, he saw Simon and his brother Andrew casting a net into the lake, for they were fishermen. [17]"Come, follow me," Jesus said, "and I will make you fishers of men." [18]At once they left their nets and followed him.

[19]When he had gone a little farther, he saw James son of Zebedee and his brother John in a boat, preparing their nets. [20]Without delay he called them, and they left their father Zebedee in the boat with the hired men and followed him.

Jesus Drives Out an Evil Spirit

[21]They went to Capernaum, and when the Sabbath came, Jesus went into the synagogue and began to teach. [22]The people were amazed at his teaching, because he taught them as one who had authority, not as the teachers of the law. [23]Just then a man in their synagogue who was possessed by an evil spirit cried out, [24]"What do you want with us, Jesus of Nazareth? Have you come to destroy us? I know who you are—the Holy One of God!"

[25]"Be quiet!" said Jesus sternly. "Come out of him!" [26]The evil spirit shook the man violently and came out of him with a shriek.

[27]The people were all so amazed that they asked each other, "What is this? A new teaching—and with authority! He even gives orders to evil spirits and they obey him." [28]News about him spread quickly over the whole region of Galilee.

Jesus Heals Many

[29]As soon as they left the synagogue, they went with James and John to the home of Simon and Andrew. [30]Simon's mother-in-law was in bed with a fever, and they told Jesus about her. [31]So he went to he;r, took her hand and helped her up. The fever left her and she began to wait on them.

[32]That evening after sunset the people brought to Jesus all the sick and demon-possessed. [33]The whole town gathered at the door, [34]and Jesus healed many who had various diseases. He also drove out many demons, but he would not let the demons speak because they knew who he was.

Jesus Prays in a Solitary Place

[35]Very early in the morning, while it was still dark, Jesus got up, left the house and went off to a solitary place, where he prayed. [36]Simon and his companions went to look for him, [37]and when they found him, they exclaimed: "Everyone is looking for you!"

[38]Jesus replied, "Let us go somewhere else—to the nearby villages—so I can preach there also. That is why I have come." [39]So he traveled throughout Galilee, preaching in their synagogues and driving out demons.

A Man With Leprosy

[40]A man with leprosy came to him and begged him on his knees, "If you are willing, you can make me clean."

[41]Filled with compassion, Jesus reached out his hand and touched the man. "I am willing," he said. "Be clean!" [42]Immediately the leprosy left him and he was cured.

[43]Jesus sent him away at once with a strong warning: [44]"See that you don't tell this to anyone. But go, show yourself to the priest and offer the sacrifices that Moses commanded for your cleansing, as a testimony to them." [45]Instead he went out and began to talk freely, spreading the news. As a result, Jesus could no longer enter a town openly but stayed outside in lonely places. Yet the people still came to him from everywhere.

Jesus Heals a Paralytic

2 A few days later, when Jesus again entered Capernaum, the people heard that he had come home. [2]So many gathered that there was no room left, not even outside the door, and he preached the word to them. [3]Some men came, bringing to him a paralytic, carried by four of them. [4]Since they could not get him to Jesus because of the crowd, they made an opening in the roof above Jesus and, after digging through it, lowered the mat the paralyzed man was lying on. [5]When Jesus saw their faith, he said to the paralytic, "Son, your sins are forgiven."

[6]Now some teachers of the law were sitting there, thinking to themselves, [7]"Why does this fellow talk like that? He's blaspheming! Who can forgive sins but God alone?"

[8]Immediately Jesus knew in his spirit that this was what they were thinking in their hearts, and he said to them, "Why are you thinking these things? [9]Which is easier: to say to the paralytic, 'Your sins are forgiven,' or to say, 'Get up, take your mat and walk'? [10]But that you may know that the Son of Man has authority on earth to forgive sins ..." He said to the paralytic, [11]"I tell you, get up, take your mat and go home." [12]He got up, took his mat and walked out in full view of them all. This amazed everyone and they praised God, saying, "We have never seen anything like this!"

The Calling of Levi

[13]Once again Jesus went out beside the lake. A large crowd came to him, and he began to teach them. [14]As he walked along, he saw Levi son of Alphaeus

sitting at the tax collector's booth. "Follow me," Jesus told him, and Levi got up and followed him.

[15]While Jesus was having dinner at Levi's house, many tax collectors and "sinners" were eating with him and his disciples, for there were many who followed him. [16]When the teachers of the law who were Pharisees saw him eating with the "sinners" and tax collectors, they asked his disciples: "Why does he eat with tax collectors and 'sinners'?"

[17]On hearing this, Jesus said to them, "It is not the healthy who need a doctor, but the sick. I have not come to call the righteous, but sinners."

Jesus Questioned About Fasting

[18]Now John's disciples and the Pharisees were fasting. Some people came and asked Jesus, "How is it that John's disciples and the disciples of the Pharisees are fasting, but yours are not?"

[19]Jesus answered, "How can the guests of the bridegroom fast while he is with them? They cannot, so long as they have him with them. [20]But the time will come when the bridegroom will be taken from them, and on that day they will fast.

[21]"No one sews a patch of unshrunk cloth on an old garment. If he does, the new piece will pull away from the old, making the tear worse. [22]And no one pours new wine into old wineskins. If he does, the wine will burst the skins, and both the wine and the wineskins will be ruined. No, he pours new wine into new wineskins."

Lord of the Sabbath

[23]One Sabbath Jesus was going through the grainfields, and as his disciples walked along, they began to pick some heads of grain. [24]The Pharisees said to him, "Look, why are they doing what is unlawful on the Sabbath?"

[25]He answered, "Have you never read what David did when he and his companions were hungry and in need? [26]In the days of Abiathar the high priest, he entered the house of God and ate the consecrated bread, which is lawful only for priests to eat. And he also gave some to his companions."

[27]Then he said to them, "The Sabbath was made for man, not man for the Sabbath. [28]So the Son of Man is Lord even of the Sabbath."

3 Another time he went into the synagogue, and a man with a shriveled hand was there. [2]Some of them were looking for a reason to accuse Jesus, so they watched him closely to see if he would heal him on the Sabbath. [3]Jesus said to the man with the shriveled hand, "Stand up in front of everyone."

[4]Then Jesus asked them, "Which is lawful on the Sabbath: to do good or to do evil, to save life or to kill?" But they remained silent.

[5]He looked around at them in anger and, deeply distressed at their stubborn hearts, said to the man, "Stretch out your hand." He stretched it out, and his hand was completely restored. [6]Then the Pharisees went out and began to plot with the Herodians how they might kill Jesus.

Crowds Follow Jesus

[7]Jesus withdrew with his disciples to the lake, and a large crowd from Galilee followed. [8]When they heard all he was doing, many people came to him from Judea, Jerusalem, Idumea, and the regions across the Jordan and around Tyre and Sidon. [9]Because of the crowd he told his disciples to have a small boat ready for him, to keep the people from crowding him. [10]For he had healed many, so that those with diseases were pushing forward to touch him. [11]Whenever the evil spirits saw him, they fell down before him and cried out, "You are the Son of God." [12]But he gave them strict orders not to tell who he was.

The Appointing of the Twelve Apostles

[13]Jesus went up on a mountainside and called to him those he wanted, and they came to him. [14]He appointed twelve—designating them apostles—that they might be with him and that he might send them out to preach [15]and to have authority to drive out demons. [16]These are the twelve he appointed: Simon (to whom he gave the name Peter); [17]James son of Zebedee and his brother John (to them he gave the name Boanerges, which means Sons of Thunder); [18]Andrew, Philip, Bartholomew, Matthew, Thomas, James son of Alphaeus, Thaddaeus, Simon the Zealot [19]and Judas Iscariot, who betrayed him.

Jesus and Beelzebub

[20]Then Jesus entered a house, and again a crowd gathered, so that he and his disciples were not even able to eat. [21]When his family heard about this, they went to take charge of him, for they said, "He is out of his mind."

[22]And the teachers of the law who came down from Jerusalem said, "He is possessed by Beelzebub! By the prince of demons he is driving out demons."

[23]So Jesus called them and spoke to them in parables: "How can Satan drive out Satan? [24]If a kingdom is divided against itself, that kingdom cannot stand. [25]If a house is divided against itself, that house cannot stand. [26]And if Satan opposes himself and is divided, he cannot stand; his end has come. [27]In fact, no one can enter a strong man's house and carry off his possessions unless he first ties up the strong man. Then he can rob his house. [28]I tell you the truth, all the sins and blasphemies of men will be forgiven them. [29]But whoever blasphemes against the Holy Spirit will never be forgiven; he is guilty of an eternal sin."

[30]He said this because they were saying, "He has an evil spirit."

Jesus' Mother and Brothers

[31]Then Jesus' mother and brothers arrived. Standing outside, they sent someone in to call him. [32]A crowd was sitting around him, and they told him, "Your mother and brothers are outside looking for you."

[33]"Who are my mother and my brothers?" he asked.

[34]Then he looked at those seated in a circle around him and said, "Here are my mother and my brothers! [35]Whoever does God's will is my brother and sister and mother."

The Parable of the Sower

4 Again Jesus began to teach by the lake. The crowd that gathered around him was so large that he got into a boat and sat in it out on the lake, while all the people were along the shore at the water's edge. [2]He taught them many things by parables, and in his teaching said: [3]"Listen! A farmer went out to sow his seed. [4]As he was scattering the seed, some fell along the path, and the birds came and ate it up. [5]Some fell on rocky places, where it did not have much soil. It sprang up quickly, because the soil was shallow. [6]But when the sun came up, the plants were scorched, and they withered because they had no root. [7]Other seed fell among thorns, which grew up and choked the plants, so that they did not bear grain. [8]Still other seed fell on good soil. It came up, grew and produced a crop, multiplying thirty, sixty, or even a hundred times."

[9]Then Jesus said, "He who has ears to hear, let him hear."

[10]When he was alone, the Twelve and the others around him asked him about the parables. [11]He told them, "The secret of the kingdom of God has been given to you. But to those on the outside everything is said in parables [12]so that,

> "'they may be ever seeing but never perceiving,
> and ever hearing but never understanding;
> otherwise they might turn and be forgiven!'"

[13]Then Jesus said to them, "Don't you understand this parable? How then will you understand any parable? [14]The farmer sows the word. [15]Some people are like seed along the path, where the word is sown. As soon as they hear it, Satan comes and takes away the word that was sown in them. [16]Others, like seed sown on rocky places, hear the word and at once receive it with joy. [17]But since they have no root, they last only a short time. When trouble or persecution comes because of the word, they quickly fall away. [18]Still others, like seed sown among thorns, hear the word; [19]but the worries of this life, the deceitfulness of wealth and the desires for other things come in and choke the word, making it unfruitful. [20]Others, like seed sown on good soil, hear the word,

accept it, and produce a crop—thirty, sixty or even a hundred times what was sown."

A Lamp on a Stand

[21]He said to them, "Do you bring in a lamp to put it under a bowl or a bed? Instead, don't you put it on its stand? [22]For whatever is hidden is meant to be disclosed, and whatever is concealed is meant to be brought out into the open. [23]If anyone has ears to hear, let him hear."

[24]"Consider carefully what you hear," he continued. "With the measure you use, it will be measured to you—and even more. [25]Whoever has will be given more; whoever does not have, even what he has will be taken from him."

The Parable of the Growing Seed

[26]He also said, "This is what the kingdom of God is like. A man scatters seed on the ground. [27]Night and day, whether he sleeps or gets up, the seed sprouts and grows, though he does not know how. [28]All by itself the soil produces grain—first the stalk, then the head, then the full kernel in the head. [29]As soon as the grain is ripe, he puts the sickle to it, because the harvest has come."

The Parable of the Mustard Seed

[30]Again he said, "What shall we say the kingdom of God is like, or what parable shall we use to describe it? [31]It is like a mustard seed, which is the smallest seed you plant in the ground. [32]Yet when planted, it grows and becomes the largest of all garden plants, with such big branches that the birds of the air can perch in its shade."

[33]With many similar parables Jesus spoke the word to them, as much as they could understand. [34]He did not say anything to them without using a parable. But when he was alone with his own disciples, he explained everything.

Jesus Calms the Storm

[35]That day when evening came, he said to his disciples, "Let us go over to the other side." [36]Leaving the crowd behind, they took him along, just as he was, in the boat. There were also other boats with him. [37]A furious squall came up, and the waves broke over the boat, so that it was nearly swamped. [38]Jesus was in the stern, sleeping on a cushion. The disciples woke him and said to him, "Teacher, don't you care if we drown?"

[39]He got up, rebuked the wind and said to the waves, "Quiet! Be still!" Then the wind died down and it was completely calm.

[40]He said to his disciples, "Why are you so afraid? Do you still have no faith?"

[41]They were terrified and asked each other, "Who is this? Even the wind and the waves obey him!"

The Healing of a Demon-possessed Man

5 They went across the lake to the region of the Gerasenes. [2]When Jesus got out of the boat, a man with an evil spirit came from the tombs to meet him. [3]This man lived in the tombs, and no one could bind him any more, not even with a chain. [4]For he had often been chained hand and foot, but he tore the chains apart and broke the irons on his feet. No one was strong enough to subdue him. [5]Night and day among the tombs and in the hills he would cry out and cut himself with stones.

[6]When he saw Jesus from a distance, he ran and fell on his knees in front of him. [7]He shouted at the top of his voice, "What do you want with me, Jesus, Son of the Most High God? Swear to God that you won't torture me!" [8]For Jesus had said to him, "Come out of this man, you evil spirit!"

[9]Then Jesus asked him, "What is your name?"

"My name is Legion," he replied, "for we are many." [10]And he begged Jesus again and again not to send them out of the area.

[11]A large herd of pigs was feeding on the nearby hillside. [12]The demons begged Jesus, "Send us among the pigs; allow us to go into them." [13]He gave them permission, and the evil spirits came out and went into the pigs. The herd, about two thousand in number, rushed down the steep bank into the lake and were drowned.

[14]Those tending the pigs ran off and reported this in the town and countryside, and the people went out to see what had happened. [15]When they came to Jesus, they saw the man who had been possessed by the legion of demons, sitting there, dressed and in his right mind; and they were afraid. [16]Those who had seen it told the people what had happened to the demon-possessed man—and told about the pigs as well. [17]Then the people began to plead with Jesus to leave their region.

[18]As Jesus was getting into the boat, the man who had been demon-possessed begged to go with him. [19]Jesus did not let him, but said, "Go home to your family and tell them how much the Lord has done for you, and how he has had mercy on you." [20]So the man went away and began to tell in the Decapolis how much Jesus had done for him. And all the people were amazed.

A Dead Girl and a Sick Woman

[21]When Jesus had again crossed over by boat to the other side of the lake, a large crowd gathered around him while he was by the lake. [22]Then one of the synagogue rulers, named Jairus, came there. Seeing Jesus, he fell at his feet [23]and pleaded earnestly with him, "My little daughter is dying. Please come and put your hands on her so that she will be healed and live." [24]So Jesus went with him.

A large crowd followed and pressed around him. [25]And a woman was there who had been subject to bleeding for twelve years. [26]She had suffered a great deal under the care of many doctors and had spent all she had, yet instead of getting better she grew worse. [27]When she heard about Jesus, she came up behind him in the crowd and touched his cloak, [28]because she thought, "If I just touch his clothes, I will be healed." [29]Immediately her bleeding stopped and she felt in her body that she was freed from her suffering.

[30]At once Jesus realized that power had gone out from him. He turned around in the crowd and asked, "Who touched my clothes?"

[31]"You see the people crowding against you," his disciples answered, "and yet you can ask, 'Who touched me?'"

[32]But Jesus kept looking around to see who had done it. [33]Then the woman, knowing what had happened to her, came and fell at his feet and, trembling with fear, told him the whole truth. [34]He said to her, "Daughter, your faith has healed you. Go in peace and be freed from your suffering."

[35]While Jesus was still speaking, some men came from the house of Jairus, the synagogue ruler. "Your daughter is dead," they said. "Why bother the teacher any more?"

[36]Ignoring what they said, Jesus told the synagogue ruler, "Don't be afraid; just believe."

[37]He did not let anyone follow him except Peter, James and John the brother of James. [38]When they came to the home of the synagogue ruler, Jesus saw a commotion, with people crying and wailing loudly. [39]He went in and said to them, "Why all this commotion and wailing? The child is not dead but asleep." [40]But they laughed at him.

After he put them all out, he took the child's father and mother and the disciples who were with him, and went in where the child was. [41]He took her by the hand and said to her, *Talitha koum!*" (which means, "Little girl, I say to you, get up!"). [42]Immediately the girl stood up and walked around (she was twelve years old). At this they were completely astonished. [43]He gave strict orders not to let anyone know about this, and told them to give her something to eat.

A Prophet Without Honor

6 Jesus left there and went to his hometown, accompanied by his disciples. [2]When the Sabbath came, he began to teach in the synagogue, and many who heard him were amazed.

"Where did this man get these things?" they asked. "What's this wisdom that has been given him, that he even does miracles! [3]Isn't this the carpenter? Isn't this Mary's son and the brother of James, Joseph, Judas and Simon? Aren't his sisters here with us?" And they took offense at him.

[4]Jesus said to them, "Only in his hometown, among his relatives and in his own house is a prophet without honor." [5]He could not do any miracles there, except lay his hands on a few sick people and heal them. [6]And he was amazed at their lack of faith.

Jesus Sends Out the Twelve

Then Jesus went around teaching from village to village. [7]Calling the Twelve to him, he sent them out two by two and gave them authority over evil spirits.

[8]These were his instructions: "Take nothing for the journey except a staff— no bread, no bag, no money in your belts. [9]Wear sandals but not an extra tunic. [10]Whenever you enter a house, stay there until you leave that town. [11]And if any place will not welcome you or listen to you, shake the dust off your feet when you leave, as a testimony against them."

[12]They went out and preached that people should repent. [13]They drove out many demons and anointed many sick people with oil and healed them.

John the Baptist Beheaded

[14]King Herod heard about this, for Jesus' name had become well known. Some were saying, "John the Baptist has been raised from the dead, and that is why miraculous powers are at work in him."

[15]Others said, "He is Elijah."

And still others claimed, "He is a prophet, like one of the prophets of long ago."

[16]But when Herod heard this, he said, "John, the man I beheaded, has been raised from the dead!"

[17]For Herod himself had given orders to have John arrested, and he had him bound and put in prison. He did this because of Herodias, his brother Philip's wife, whom he had married. [18]For John had been saying to Herod, "It is not lawful for you to have your brother's wife." [19]So Herodias nursed a grudge against John and wanted to kill him. But she was not able to, [20]because Herod feared John and protected him, knowing him to be a righteous and holy man. When Herod heard John, he was greatly puzzled; yet he liked to listen to him.

[21]Finally the opportune time came. On his birthday Herod gave a banquet for his high officials and military commanders and the leading men of Galilee. [22]When the daughter of Herodias came in and danced, she pleased Herod and his dinner guests.

The king said to the girl, "Ask me for anything you want, and I'll give it to you." [23]And he promised her with an oath, "Whatever you ask I will give you, up to half my kingdom."

[24]She went out and said to her mother, "What shall I ask for?"

"The head of John the Baptist," she answered.

[25]At once the girl hurried in to the king with the request: "I want you to give me right now the head of John the Baptist on a platter." [26]The king was greatly distressed, but because of his oaths and his dinner guests, he did not want to refuse her. [27]So he immediately sent an executioner with orders to bring John's head. The man went, beheaded John in the prison, [28]and brought back his head on a platter. He presented it to the girl, and she gave it to her mother. [29]On hearing of this, John's disciples came and took his body and laid it in a tomb.

Jesus Feeds the Five Thousand

[30]The apostles gathered around Jesus and reported to him all they had done and taught. [31]Then, because so many people were coming and going that they did not even have a chance to eat, he said to them, "Come with me by yourselves to a quiet place and get some rest."

[32]So they went away by themselves in a boat to a solitary place. [33]But many who saw them leaving recognized them and ran on foot from all the towns and got there ahead of them. [34]When Jesus landed and saw a large crowd, he had compassion on them, because they were like sheep without a shepherd. So he began teaching them many things.

[35]By this time it was late in the day, so his disciples came to him. "This is a remote place," they said, "and it's already very late. [36]Send the people away so they can go to the surrounding countryside and villages and buy themselves something to eat."

[37]But he answered, "You give them something to eat."

They said to him, "That would take eight months of a man's wages! Are we to go and spend that much on bread and give it to them to eat?"

[38]"How many loaves do you have?" he asked. "Go and see."

When they found out, they said, "Five—and two fish."

[39]Then Jesus directed them to have all the people sit down in groups on the green grass. [40]So they sat down in groups of hundreds and fifties. [41]Taking the five loaves and the two fish and looking up to heaven, he gave thanks and broke the loaves. Then he gave them to his disciples to set before the people. He also divided the two fish among them all. [42]They all ate and were satisfied, [43]and the disciples picked up twelve basketfuls of broken pieces of bread and fish. [44]The number of the men who had eaten was five thousand.

Jesus Walks on the Water

[45]Immediately Jesus made his disciples get into the boat and go on ahead of him to Bethsaida, while he dismissed the crowd. [46]After leaving them, he went up on a mountainside to pray.

⁴⁷When evening came, the boat was in the middle of the lake, and he was alone on land. ⁴⁸He saw the disciples straining at the oars, because the wind was against them. About the fourth watch of the night he went out to them, walking on the lake. He was about to pass by them, ⁴⁹but when they saw him walking on the lake, they thought he was a ghost. They cried out, ⁵⁰because they all saw him and were terrified.

Immediately he spoke to them and said, "Take courage! It is I. Don't be afraid." ⁵¹Then he climbed into the boat with them, and the wind died down. They were completely amazed, ⁵²for they had not understood about the loaves; their hearts were hardened.

⁵³When they had crossed over, they landed at Gennesaret and anchored there. ⁵⁴As soon as they got out of the boat, people recognized Jesus. ⁵⁵They ran throughout that whole region and carried the sick on mats to wherever they heard he was. ⁵⁶And wherever he went—into villages, towns or countryside—they placed the sick in the marketplaces. They begged him to let them touch even the edge of his cloak, and all who touched him were healed.

Clean and Unclean

7 The Pharisees and some of the teachers of the law who had come from Jerusalem gathered around Jesus and ²saw some of his disciples eating food with hands that were "unclean," that is, unwashed. ³(The Pharisees and all the Jews do not eat unless they give their hands a ceremonial washing, holding to the tradition of the elders. ⁴When they come from the marketplace they do not eat unless they wash. And they observe many other traditions, such as the washing of cups, pitchers and kettles.)

⁵So the Pharisees and teachers of the law asked Jesus, "Why don't your disciples live according to the tradition of the elders instead of eating their food with 'unclean' hands?"

⁶He replied, "Isaiah was right when he prophesied about you hypocrites; as it is written:

"'These people honor me with their lips,
   but their hearts are far from me.
⁷They worship me in vain;
   their teachings are but rules taught by men.'
⁸You have let go of the commands of God and are holding on to the
   traditions of men."

⁹And he said to them: "You have a fine way of setting aside the commands of God in order to observe your own traditions! ¹⁰For Moses said, 'Honor your father and your mother,' and, 'Anyone who curses his father or mother must be

put to death.' [11]But you say that if a man says to his father or mother: 'Whatever help you might otherwise have received from me is Corban' (that is, a gift devoted to God), [12]then you no longer let him do anything for his father or mother. [13]Thus you nullify the word of God by your tradition that you have handed down. And you do many things like that."

[14]Again Jesus called the crowd to him and said, "Listen to me, everyone, and understand this. [15]Nothing outside a man can make him 'unclean' by going into him. Rather, it is what comes out of a man that makes him 'unclean.'"

[17]After he had left the crowd and entered the house, his disciples asked him about this parable. [18]"Are you so dull?" he asked. "Don't you see that nothing that enters a man from the outside can make him 'unclean'? [19]For it doesn't go into his heart but into his stomach, and then out of his body." (In saying this, Jesus declared all foods "clean.")

[20]He went on: "What comes out of a man is what makes him 'unclean.' [21]For from within, out of men's hearts, come evil thoughts, sexual immorality, theft, murder, adultery, [22]greed, malice, deceit, lewdness, envy, slander, arrogance and folly. [23]All these evils come from inside and make a man 'unclean.'"

The Faith of a Syrophoenician Woman

[24]Jesus left that place and went to the vicinity of Tyre. He entered a house and did not want anyone to know it; yet he could not keep his presence secret. [25]In fact, as soon as she heard about him, a woman whose little daughter was possessed by an evil spirit came and fell at his feet. [26]The woman was a Greek, born in Syrian Phoenicia. She begged Jesus to drive the demon out of her daughter.

[27]"First let the children eat all they want," he told her, "for it is not right to take the children's bread and toss it to their dogs."

[28]"Yes, Lord," she replied, "but even the dogs under the table eat the children's crumbs."

[29]Then he told her, "For such a reply, you may go; the demon has left your daughter."

[30]She went home and found her child lying on the bed, and the demon gone.

The Healing of a Deaf and Mute Man

[31]Then Jesus left the vicinity of Tyre and went through Sidon, down to the Sea of Galilee and into the region of the Decapolis. [32]There some people brought to him a man who was deaf and could hardly talk, and they begged him to place his hand on the man.

[33]After he took him aside, away from the crowd, Jesus put his fingers into the man's ears. Then he spit and touched the man's tongue. [34]He looked up to heaven and with a deep sigh said to him, *Ephphatha!* (which means, "Be

opened!"). [35]At this, the man's ears were opened, his tongue was loosened and he began to speak plainly.

[36]Jesus commanded them not to tell anyone. But the more he did so, the more they kept talking about it. [37]People were overwhelmed with amazement. "He has done everything well," they said. "He even makes the deaf hear and the mute speak."

Jesus Feeds the Four Thousand

8 During those days another large crowd gathered. Since they had nothing to eat, Jesus called his disciples to him and said, [2]"I have compassion for these people; they have already been with me three days and have nothing to eat. [3]If I send them home hungry, they will collapse on the way, because some of them have come a long distance."

[4]His disciples answered, "But where in this remote place can anyone get enough bread to feed them?"

[5]"How many loaves do you have?" Jesus asked.

"Seven," they replied.

[6]He told the crowd to sit down on the ground. When he had taken the seven loaves and given thanks, he broke them and gave them to his disciples to set before the people, and they did so. [7]They had a few small fish as well; he gave thanks for them also and told the disciples to distribute them. [8]The people ate and were satisfied. Afterward the disciples picked up seven basketfuls of broken pieces that were left over. [9]About four thousand men were present. And having sent them away, [10]he got into the boat with his disciples and went to the region of Dalmanutha.

[11]The Pharisees came and began to question Jesus. To test him, they asked him for a sign from heaven. [12]He sighed deeply and said, "Why does this generation ask for a miraculous sign? I tell you the truth, no sign will be given to it." [13]Then he left them, got back into the boat and crossed to the other side.

The Yeast of the Pharisees and Herod

[14]The disciples had forgotten to bring bread, except for one loaf they had with them in the boat. [15]"Be careful," Jesus warned them. "Watch out for the yeast of the Pharisees and that of Herod."

[16]They discussed this with one another and said, "It is because we have no bread."

[17]Aware of their discussion, Jesus asked them: "Why are you talking about having no bread? Do you still not see or understand? Are your hearts hardened? [18]Do you have eyes but fail to see, and ears but fail to hear? And don't you remember? [19]When I broke the five loaves for the five thousand, how many basketfuls of pieces did you pick up?"

"Twelve," they replied.

[20]"And when I broke the seven loaves for the four thousand, how many basketfuls of pieces did you pick up?"

They answered, "Seven."

[21]He said to them, "Do you still not understand?"

The Healing of a Blind Man at Bethsaida

[22]They came to Bethsaida, and some people brought a blind man and begged Jesus to touch him. [23]He took the blind man by the hand and led him outside the village. When he had spit on the man's eyes and put his hands on him, Jesus asked, "Do you see anything?"

[24]He looked up and said, "I see people; they look like trees walking around."

[25]Once more Jesus put his hands on the man's eyes. Then his eyes were opened, his sight was restored, and he saw everything clearly. [26]Jesus sent him home, saying, "Don't go into the village."

Peter's Confession of Christ

[27]Jesus and his disciples went on to the villages around Caesarea Philippi. On the way he asked them, "Who do people say I am?"

[28]They replied, "Some say John the Baptist; others say Elijah; and still others, one of the prophets."

[29]"But what about you?" he asked. "Who do you say I am?"

Peter answered, "You are the Christ."

[30]Jesus warned them not to tell anyone about him.

Jesus Predicts His Death

[31]He then began to teach them that the Son of Man must suffer many things and be rejected by the elders, chief priests and teachers of the law, and that he must be killed and after three days rise again. [32]He spoke plainly about this, and Peter took him aside and began to rebuke him.

[33]But when Jesus turned and looked at his disciples, he rebuked Peter. "Get behind me, Satan!" he said. "You do not have in mind the things of God, but the things of men."

[34]Then he called the crowd to him along with his disciples and said: "If anyone would come after me, he must deny himself and take up his cross and follow me. [35]For whoever wants to save his life will lose it, but whoever loses his life for me and for the gospel will save it. [36]What good is it for a man to gain the whole world, yet forfeit his soul? [37]Or what can a man give in exchange for his soul? [38]If anyone is ashamed of me and my words in this adulterous and sinful generation, the Son of Man will be ashamed of him when he comes in his Father's glory with the holy angels."

9And he said to them, "I tell you the truth, some who are standing here will not taste death before they see the kingdom of God come with power."

The Transfiguration

[2]After six days Jesus took Peter, James and John with him and led them up a high mountain, where they were all alone. There he was transfigured before them. [3]His clothes became dazzling white, whiter than anyone in the world could bleach them. [4]And there appeared before them Elijah and Moses, who were talking with Jesus.

[5]Peter said to Jesus, "Rabbi, it is good for us to be here. Let us put up three shelters—one for you, one for Moses and one for Elijah." [6](He did not know what to say, they were so frightened.)

[7]Then a cloud appeared and enveloped them, and a voice came from the cloud: "This is my Son, whom I love. Listen to him!"

[8]Suddenly, when they looked around, they no longer saw anyone with them except Jesus.

[9]As they were coming down the mountain, Jesus gave them orders not to tell anyone what they had seen until the Son of Man had risen from the dead. [10]They kept the matter to themselves, discussing what "rising from the dead" meant.

[11]And they asked him, "Why do the teachers of the law say that Elijah must come first?"

[12]Jesus replied, "To be sure, Elijah does come first, and restores all things. Why then is it written that the Son of Man must suffer much and be rejected? [13]But I tell you, Elijah has come, and they have done to him everything they wished, just as it is written about him."

The Healing of a Boy With an Evil Spirit

[14]When they came to the other disciples, they saw a large crowd around them and the teachers of the law arguing with them. [15]As soon as all the people saw Jesus, they were overwhelmed with wonder and ran to greet him.

[16]"What are you arguing with them about?" he asked.

[17]A man in the crowd answered, "Teacher, I brought you my son, who is possessed by a spirit that has robbed him of speech. [18]Whenever it seizes him, it throws him to the ground. He foams at the mouth, gnashes his teeth and becomes rigid. I asked your disciples to drive out the spirit, but they could not."

[19]"O unbelieving generation," Jesus replied, "how long shall I stay with you? How long shall I put up with you? Bring the boy to me."

20So they brought him. When the spirit saw Jesus, it immediately threw the boy into a convulsion. He fell to the ground and rolled around, foaming at the mouth.

21Jesus asked the boy's father, "How long has he been like this?"

"From childhood," he answered. 22"It has often thrown him into fire or water to kill him. But if you can do anything, take pity on us and help us."

23"'If you can'?" said Jesus. "Everything is possible for him who believes."

24Immediately the boy's father exclaimed, "I do believe; help me overcome my unbelief!"

25When Jesus saw that a crowd was running to the scene, he rebuked the evil spirit. "You deaf and mute spirit," he said, "I command you, come out of him and never enter him again."

26The spirit shrieked, convulsed him violently and came out. The boy looked so much like a corpse that many said, "He's dead." 27But Jesus took him by the hand and lifted him to his feet, and he stood up.

28After Jesus had gone indoors, his disciples asked him privately, "Why couldn't we drive it out?"

29He replied, "This kind can come out only by prayer."

30They left that place and passed through Galilee. Jesus did not want anyone to know where they were, 31because he was teaching his disciples. He said to them, "The Son of Man is going to be betrayed into the hands of men. They will kill him, and after three days he will rise." 32But they did not understand what he meant and were afraid to ask him about it.

Who Is the Greatest?

33They came to Capernaum. When he was in the house, he asked them, "What were you arguing about on the road?" 34But they kept quiet because on the way they had argued about who was the greatest.

35Sitting down, Jesus called the Twelve and said, "If anyone wants to be first, he must be the very last, and the servant of all."

36He took a little child and had him stand among them. Taking him in his arms, he said to them, 37"Whoever welcomes one of these little children in my name welcomes me; and whoever welcomes me does not welcome me but the one who sent me."

Whoever Is Not Against Us Is for Us

38"Teacher," said John, "we saw a man driving out demons in your name and we told him to stop, because he was not one of us."

39"Do not stop him," Jesus said. "No one who does a miracle in my name can in the next moment say anything bad about me, 40for whoever is not against us is for us. [41]I tell you the truth, anyone who gives you a cup of water in my name because you belong to Christ will certainly not lose his reward.

Causing to Sin

[42]"And if anyone causes one of these little ones who believe in me to sin, it would be better for him to be thrown into the sea with a large millstone tied around his neck. [43]If your hand causes you to sin, cut it off. It is better for you to enter life maimed than with two hands to go into hell, where the fire never goes out. [45]And if your foot causes you to sin, cut it off. It is better for you to enter life crippled than to have two feet and be thrown into hell. [47]And if your eye causes you to sin, pluck it out. It is better for you to enter the kingdom of God with one eye than to have two eyes and be thrown into hell, [48]where

"'their worm does not die,
and the fire is not quenched.'

[49]Everyone will be salted with fire.
[50]"Salt is good, but if it loses its saltiness, how can you make it salty again? Have salt in yourselves, and be at peace with each other."

Divorce

10 Jesus then left that place and went into the region of Judea and across the Jordan. Again crowds of people came to him, and as was his custom, he taught them.
[2]Some Pharisees came and tested him by asking, "Is it lawful for a man to divorce his wife?"
[3]"What did Moses command you?" he replied.
[4]They said, "Moses permitted a man to write a certificate of divorce and send her away."
[5]"It was because your hearts were hard that Moses wrote you this law," Jesus replied. [6]"But at the beginning of creation God 'made them male and female.' [7]For this reason a man will leave his father and mother and be united to his wife, [8]and the two will become one flesh.' So they are no longer two, but one. [9]Therefore what God has joined together, let man not separate."
[10]When they were in the house again, the disciples asked Jesus about this. [11]He answered, "Anyone who divorces his wife and marries another woman commits adultery against her. [12]And if she divorces her husband and marries another man, she commits adultery."

The Little Children and Jesus

[13]People were bringing little children to Jesus to have him touch them, but the disciples rebuked them. [14]When Jesus saw this, he was indignant. He said to them, "Let the little children come to me, and do not hinder them, for the

kingdom of God belongs to such as these. [15]I tell you the truth, anyone who will not receive the kingdom of God like a little child will never enter it." [16]And he took the children in his arms, put his hands on them and blessed them.

The Rich Young Man

[17]As Jesus started on his way, a man ran up to him and fell on his knees before him. "Good teacher," he asked, "what must I do to inherit eternal life?"

[18]"Why do you call me good?" Jesus answered. "No one is good—except God alone. [19]You know the commandments: 'Do not murder, do not commit adultery, do not steal, do not give false testimony, do not defraud, honor your father and mother.'"

[20]"Teacher," he declared, "all these I have kept since I was a boy."

[21]Jesus looked at him and loved him. "One thing you lack," he said. "Go, sell everything you have and give to the poor, and you will have treasure in heaven. Then come, follow me."

[22]At this the man's face fell. He went away sad, because he had great wealth.

[23]Jesus looked around and said to his disciples, "How hard it is for the rich to enter the kingdom of God!"

[24]The disciples were amazed at his words. But Jesus said again, "Children, how hard it is to enter the kingdom of God! [25]It is easier for a camel to go through the eye of a needle than for a rich man to enter the kingdom of God."

[26]The disciples were even more amazed, and said to each other, "Who then can be saved?"

[27]Jesus looked at them and said, "With man this is impossible, but not with God; all things are possible with God."

[28]Peter said to him, "We have left everything to follow you!"

[29]"I tell you the truth," Jesus replied, "no one who has left home or brothers or sisters or mother or father or children or fields for me and the gospel [30]will fail to receive a hundred times as much in this present age (homes, brothers, sisters, mothers, children and fields—and with them, persecutions) and in the age to come, eternal life. [31]But many who are first will be last, and the last first."

Jesus Again Predicts His Death

[32]They were on their way up to Jerusalem, with Jesus leading the way, and the disciples were astonished, while those who followed were afraid. Again he took the Twelve aside and told them what was going to happen to him. [33]"We are going up to Jerusalem," he said, "and the Son of Man will be betrayed to the chief priests and teachers of the law. They will condemn him to death and will hand him over to the Gentiles, [34]who will mock him and spit on him, flog him and kill him. Three days later he will rise."

The Request of James and John

[35]Then James and John, the sons of Zebedee, came to him. "Teacher," they said, "we want you to do for us whatever we ask."

[36]"What do you want me to do for you?" he asked.

[37]They replied, "Let one of us sit at your right and the other at your left in your glory."

[38]"You don't know what you are asking," Jesus said. "Can you drink the cup I drink or be baptized with the baptism I am baptized with?"

[39]"We can," they answered.

Jesus said to them, "You will drink the cup I drink and be baptized with the baptism I am baptized with, [40]but to sit at my right or left is not for me to grant. These places belong to those for whom they have been prepared."

[41]When the ten heard about this, they became indignant with James and John. [42]Jesus called them together and said, "You know that those who are regarded as rulers of the Gentiles lord it over them, and their high officials exercise authority over them. [43]Not so with you. Instead, whoever wants to become great among you must be your servant, [44]and whoever wants to be first must be slave of all. [45]For even the Son of Man did not come to be served, but to serve, and to give his life as a ransom for many."

Blind Bartimaeus Receives His Sight

[46]Then they came to Jericho. As Jesus and his disciples, together with a large crowd, were leaving the city, a blind man, Bartimaeus (that is, the Son of Timaeus), was sitting by the roadside begging. [47]When he heard that it was Jesus of Nazareth, he began to shout, "Jesus, Son of David, have mercy on me!"

[48]Many rebuked him and told him to be quiet, but he shouted all the more, "Son of David, have mercy on me!"

[49]Jesus stopped and said, "Call him."

So they called to the blind man, "Cheer up! On your feet! He's calling you." [50]Throwing his cloak aside, he jumped to his feet and came to Jesus.

[51]"What do you want me to do for you?" Jesus asked him.

The blind man said, "Rabbi, I want to see."

[52]"Go," said Jesus, "your faith has healed you." Immediately he received his sight and followed Jesus along the road.

The Triumphal Entry

11 As they approached Jerusalem and came to Bethphage and Bethany at the Mount of Olives, Jesus sent two of his disciples, [2]saying to them, "Go to the village ahead of you, and just as you enter it, you will find a colt tied there, which no one has ever ridden. Untie it and bring it here. [3]If anyone asks

you, 'Why are you doing this?' tell him, 'The Lord needs it and will send it back here shortly.'"

⁴They went and found a colt outside in the street, tied at a doorway. As they untied it, ⁵some people standing there asked, "What are you doing, untying that colt?" ⁶They answered as Jesus had told them to, and the people let them go. ⁷When they brought the colt to Jesus and threw their cloaks over it, he sat on it. ⁸Many people spread their cloaks on the road, while others spread branches they had cut in the fields. ⁹Those who went ahead and those who followed shouted,

> "Hosanna!"
>
> "Blessed is he who comes in the name of the Lord!"
>
> ¹⁰"Blessed is the coming kingdom of our father David!"
>
> "Hosanna in the highest!"

¹¹Jesus entered Jerusalem and went to the temple. He looked around at everything, but since it was already late, he went out to Bethany with the Twelve.

Jesus Clears the Temple

¹²The next day as they were leaving Bethany, Jesus was hungry. ¹³Seeing in the distance a fig tree in leaf, he went to find out if it had any fruit. When he reached it, he found nothing but leaves, because it was not the season for figs. ¹⁴Then he said to the tree, "May no one ever eat fruit from you again." And his disciples heard him say it.

¹⁵On reaching Jerusalem, Jesus entered the temple area and began driving out those who were buying and selling there. He overturned the tables of the money changers and the benches of those selling doves, ¹⁶and would not allow anyone to carry merchandise through the temple courts. ¹⁷And as he taught them, he said, "Is it not written:

> "'My house will be called
> a house of prayer for all nations'?
>
> But you have made it 'a den of robbers.'"

¹⁸The chief priests and the teachers of the law heard this and began looking for a way to kill him, for they feared him, because the whole crowd was amazed at his teaching.

¹⁹When evening came, they went out of the city.

The Withered Fig Tree

²⁰In the morning, as they went along, they saw the fig tree withered from the roots. ²¹Peter remembered and said to Jesus, "Rabbi, look! The fig tree you cursed has withered!"

²²"Have faith in God," Jesus answered. ²³"I tell you the truth, if anyone says to this mountain, 'Go, throw yourself into the sea,' and does not doubt in his heart but believes that what he says will happen, it will be done for him. ²⁴Therefore I tell you, whatever you ask for in prayer, believe that you have received it, and it will be yours. ²⁵And when you stand praying, if you hold anything against anyone, forgive him, so that your Father in heaven may forgive you your sins."

The Authority of Jesus Questioned

²⁷They arrived again in Jerusalem, and while Jesus was walking in the temple courts, the chief priests, the teachers of the law and the elders came to him. ²⁸"By what authority are you doing these things?" they asked. "And who gave you authority to do this?"

²⁹Jesus replied, "I will ask you one question. Answer me, and I will tell you by what authority I am doing these things. ³⁰John's baptism—was it from heaven, or from men? Tell me!"

³¹They discussed it among themselves and said, "If we say, 'From heaven,' he will ask, 'Then why didn't you believe him?' ³²But if we say, 'From men'..." (They feared the people, for everyone held that John really was a prophet.)

³³So they answered Jesus, "We don't know."

Jesus said, "Neither will I tell you by what authority I am doing these things."

The Parable of the Tenants

12 He then began to speak to them in parables: "A man planted a vineyard. He put a wall around it, dug a pit for the winepress and built a watchtower. Then he rented the vineyard to some farmers and went away on a journey. ²At harvest time he sent a servant to the tenants to collect from them some of the fruit of the vineyard. ³But they seized him, beat him and sent him away empty-handed. ⁴Then he sent another servant to them; they struck this man on the head and treated him shamefully. ⁵He sent still another, and that one they killed. He sent many others; some of them they beat, others they killed.

⁶"He had one left to send, a son, whom he loved. He sent him last of all, saying, 'They will respect my son.'

⁷"But the tenants said to one another, 'This is the heir. Come, let's kill him, and the inheritance will be ours.' ⁸So they took him and killed him, and threw him out of the vineyard.

⁹"What then will the owner of the vineyard do? He will come and kill those tenants and give the vineyard to others. ¹⁰Haven't you read this scripture:

"'The stone the builders rejected
  has become the capstone;

[11]the Lord has done this,
and it is marvelous in our eyes'?"

[12]Then they looked for a way to arrest him because they knew he had spoken the parable against them. But they were afraid of the crowd; so they left him and went away.

Paying Taxes to Caesar

[13]Later they sent some of the Pharisees and Herodians to Jesus to catch him in his words. [14]They came to him and said, "Teacher, we know you are a man of integrity. You aren't swayed by men, because you pay no attention to who they are; but you teach the way of God in accordance with the truth. Is it right to pay taxes to Caesar or not? [15]Should we pay or shouldn't we?"

But Jesus knew their hypocrisy. "Why are you trying to trap me?" he asked. "Bring me a denarius and let me look at it." [16]They brought the coin, and he asked them, "Whose portrait is this? And whose inscription?"

"Caesar's," they replied.

[17]Then Jesus said to them, "Give to Caesar what is Caesar's and to God what is God's."

And they were amazed at him.

Marriage at the Resurrection

[18]Then the Sadducees, who say there is no resurrection, came to him with a question. [19]"Teacher," they said, "Moses wrote for us that if a man's brother dies and leaves a wife but no children, the man must marry the widow and have children for his brother. [20]Now there were seven brothers. The first one married and died without leaving any children. [21]The second one married the widow, but he also died, leaving no child. It was the same with the third. [22]In fact, none of the seven left any children. Last of all, the woman died too. [23]At the resurrection whose wife will she be, since the seven were married to her?"

[24]Jesus replied, "Are you not in error because you do not know the Scriptures or the power of God? [25]When the dead rise, they will neither marry nor be given in marriage; they will be like the angels in heaven. [26]Now about the dead rising—have you not read in the book of Moses, in the account of the bush, how God said to him, 'I am the God of Abraham, the God of Isaac, and the God of Jacob'? [27]He is not the God of the dead, but of the living. You are badly mistaken!"

The Greatest Commandment

[28]One of the teachers of the law came and heard them debating. Noticing that Jesus had given them a good answer, he asked him, "Of all the commandments, which is the most important?"

[29]"The most important one," answered Jesus, "is this: 'Hear, O Israel, the Lord our God, the Lord is one. [30]Love the Lord your God with all your heart and with all your soul and with all your mind and with all your strength.' [31]The second is this: 'Love your neighbor as yourself.' There is no commandment greater than these."

[32]"Well said, teacher," the man replied. "You are right in saying that God is one and there is no other but him. [33]To love him with all your heart, with all your understanding and with all your strength, and to love your neighbor as yourself is more important than all burnt offerings and sacrifices."

[34]When Jesus saw that he had answered wisely, he said to him, "You are not far from the kingdom of God." And from then on no one dared ask him any more questions.

Whose Son Is the Christ?

[35]While Jesus was teaching in the temple courts, he asked, "How is it that the teachers of the law say that the Christ is the son of David? [36]David himself, speaking by the Holy Spirit, declared:

"'The Lord said to my Lord:
"Sit at my right hand
until I put your enemies
under your feet."'

[37]David himself calls him 'Lord.' How then can he be his son?"

The large crowd listened to him with delight.

[38]As he taught, Jesus said, "Watch out for the teachers of the law. They like to walk around in flowing robes and be greeted in the marketplaces, [39]and have the most important seats in the synagogues and the places of honor at banquets. [40]They devour widows' houses and for a show make lengthy prayers. Such men will be punished most severely."

The Widow's Offering

[41]Jesus sat down opposite the place where the offerings were put and watched the crowd putting their money into the temple treasury. Many rich people threw in large amounts. [42]But a poor widow came and put in two very small copper coins, worth only a fraction of a penny.

[43]Calling his disciples to him, Jesus said, "I tell you the truth, this poor widow has put more into the treasury than all the others. [44]They all gave out of their wealth; but she, out of her poverty, put in everything—all she had to live on."

Signs of the End of the Age

13 As he was leaving the temple, one of his disciples said to him, "Look, Teacher! What massive stones! What magnificent buildings!"

²"Do you see all these great buildings?" replied Jesus. "Not one stone here will be left on another; every one will be thrown down."

³As Jesus was sitting on the Mount of Olives opposite the temple, Peter, James, John and Andrew asked him privately, ⁴"Tell us, when will these things happen? And what will be the sign that they are all about to be fulfilled?"

⁵Jesus said to them: "Watch out that no one deceives you. ⁶Many will come in my name, claiming, 'I am he,' and will deceive many. ⁷When you hear of wars and rumors of wars, do not be alarmed. Such things must happen, but the end is still to come. ⁸Nation will rise against nation, and kingdom against kingdom. There will be earthquakes in various places, and famines. These are the beginning of birth pains.

⁹"You must be on your guard. You will be handed over to the local councils and flogged in the synagogues. On account of me you will stand before governors and kings as witnesses to them. ¹⁰And the gospel must first be preached to all nations. ¹¹Whenever you are arrested and brought to trial, do not worry beforehand about what to say. Just say whatever is given you at the time, for it is not you speaking, but the Holy Spirit.

¹²"Brother will betray brother to death, and a father his child. Children will rebel against their parents and have them put to death. ¹³All men will hate you because of me, but he who stands firm to the end will be saved.

¹⁴"When you see 'the abomination that causes desolation' standing where it does not belong—let the reader understand—then let those who are in Judea flee to the mountains. ¹⁵Let no one on the roof of his house go down or enter the house to take anything out. ¹⁶Let no one in the field go back to get his cloak. ¹⁷How dreadful it will be in those days for pregnant women and nursing mothers! ¹⁸Pray that this will not take place in winter, ¹⁹because those will be days of distress unequaled from the beginning, when God created the world, until now—and never to be equaled again. ²⁰If the Lord had not cut short those days, no one would survive. But for the sake of the elect, whom he has chosen, he has shortened them. ²¹At that time if anyone says to you, 'Look, here is the Christ!' or, 'Look, there he is!' do not believe it. ²²For false Christs and false prophets will appear and perform signs and miracles to deceive the elect—if that were possible. ²³So be on your guard; I have told you everything ahead of time.

²⁴"But in those days, following that distress,

> "'the sun will be darkened,
>   and the moon will not give its light;
> ²⁵the stars will fall from the sky,
>   and the heavenly bodies will be shaken.'

[26]"At that time men will see the Son of Man coming in clouds with great power and glory. [27]And he will send his angels and gather his elect from the four winds, from the ends of the earth to the ends of the heavens.

[28]"Now learn this lesson from the fig tree: As soon as its twigs get tender and its leaves come out, you know that summer is near. [29]Even so, when you see these things happening, you know that it is near, right at the door. [30]I tell you the truth, this generation will certainly not pass away until all these things have happened. [31]Heaven and earth will pass away, but my words will never pass away.

The Day and Hour Unknown

[32]"No one knows about that day or hour, not even the angels in heaven, nor the Son, but only the Father. [33]Be on guard! Be alert! You do not know when that time will come. [34]It's like a man going away: He leaves his house and puts his servants in charge, each with his assigned task, and tells the one at the door to keep watch.

[35]"Therefore keep watch because you do not know when the owner of the house will come back—whether in the evening, or at midnight, or when the rooster crows, or at dawn. [36]If he comes suddenly, do not let him find you sleeping. [37]What I say to you, I say to everyone: 'Watch!'"

Jesus Anointed at Bethany

14 Now the Passover and the Feast of Unleavened Bread were only two days away, and the chief priests and the teachers of the law were looking for some sly way to arrest Jesus and kill him. [2]"But not during the Feast," they said, "or the people may riot."

[3]While he was in Bethany, reclining at the table in the home of a man known as Simon the Leper, a woman came with an alabaster jar of very expensive perfume, made of pure nard. She broke the jar and poured the perfume on his head.

[4]Some of those present were saying indignantly to one another, "Why this waste of perfume? [5]It could have been sold for more than a year's wages and the money given to the poor." And they rebuked her harshly.

[6]"Leave her alone," said Jesus. "Why are you bothering her? She has done a beautiful thing to me. [7]The poor you will always have with you, and you can help them any time you want. But you will not always have me. [8]She did what she could. She poured perfume on my body beforehand to prepare for my burial. [9]I tell you the truth, wherever the gospel is preached throughout the world, what she has done will also be told, in memory of her."

[10]Then Judas Iscariot, one of the Twelve, went to the chief priests to betray Jesus to them. [11]They were delighted to hear this and promised to give him money. So he watched for an opportunity to hand him over.

The Lord's Supper

[12]On the first day of the Feast of Unleavened Bread, when it was customary to sacrifice the Passover lamb, Jesus' disciples asked him, "Where do you want us to go and make preparations for you to eat the Passover?"

[13]So he sent two of his disciples, telling them, "Go into the city, and a man carrying a jar of water will meet you. Follow him. [14]Say to the owner of the house he enters, 'The Teacher asks: Where is my guest room, where I may eat the Passover with my disciples?' [15]He will show you a large upper room, furnished and ready. Make preparations for us there."

[16]The disciples left, went into the city and found things just as Jesus had told them. So they prepared the Passover.

[17]When evening came, Jesus arrived with the Twelve. [18]While they were reclining at the table eating, he said, "I tell you the truth, one of you will betray me—one who is eating with me."

[19]They were saddened, and one by one they said to him, "Surely not I?"

[20]"It is one of the Twelve," he replied, "one who dips bread into the bowl with me. [21]The Son of Man will go just as it is written about him. But woe to that man who betrays the Son of Man! It would be better for him if he had not been born."

[22]While they were eating, Jesus took bread, gave thanks and broke it, and gave it to his disciples, saying, "Take it; this is my body."

[23]Then he took the cup, gave thanks and offered it to them, and they all drank from it.

[24]"This is my blood of the covenant, which is poured out for many," he said to them. [25]"I tell you the truth, I will not drink again of the fruit of the vine until that day when I drink it anew in the kingdom of God."

[26]When they had sung a hymn, they went out to the Mount of Olives.

Jesus Predicts Peter's Denial

[27]"You will all fall away," Jesus told them, "for it is written:

"'I will strike the shepherd, and the sheep will be scattered.'
[28]But after I have risen, I will go ahead of you into Galilee."

[29]Peter declared, "Even if all fall away, I will not."

[30]"I tell you the truth," Jesus answered, "today—yes, tonight—before the rooster crows twice you yourself will disown me three times."

[31]But Peter insisted emphatically, "Even if I have to die with you, I will never disown you." And all the others said the same.

Gethsemane

[32]They went to a place called Gethsemane, and Jesus said to his disciples, "Sit here while I pray." [33]He took Peter, James and John along with him, and he began to be deeply distressed and troubled. [34]"My soul is overwhelmed with sorrow to the point of death," he said to them. "Stay here and keep watch."

[35]Going a little farther, he fell to the ground and prayed that if possible the hour might pass from him. [36]"*Abba*, Father," he said, "everything is possible for you. Take this cup from me. Yet not what I will, but what you will."

[37]Then he returned to his disciples and found them sleeping. "Simon," he said to Peter, "are you asleep? Could you not keep watch for one hour? [38]Watch and pray so that you will not fall into temptation. The spirit is willing, but the body is weak."

[39]Once more he went away and prayed the same thing. [40]When he came back, he again found them sleeping, because their eyes were heavy. They did not know what to say to him.

[41]Returning the third time, he said to them, "Are you still sleeping and resting? Enough! The hour has come. Look, the Son of Man is betrayed into the hands of sinners. [42]Rise! Let us go! Here comes my betrayer!"

Jesus Arrested

[43]Just as he was speaking, Judas, one of the Twelve, appeared. With him was a crowd armed with swords and clubs, sent from the chief priests, the teachers of the law, and the elders.

[44]Now the betrayer had arranged a signal with them: "The one I kiss is the man; arrest him and lead him away under guard." [45]Going at once to Jesus, Judas said, "Rabbi!" and kissed him. [46]The men seized Jesus and arrested him. [47]Then one of those standing near drew his sword and struck the servant of the high priest, cutting off his ear.

[48]"Am I leading a rebellion," said Jesus, "that you have come out with swords and clubs to capture me? [49]Every day I was with you, teaching in the temple courts, and you did not arrest me. But the Scriptures must be fulfilled." [50]Then everyone deserted him and fled.

[51]A young man, wearing nothing but a linen garment, was following Jesus. When they seized him, [52]he fled naked, leaving his garment behind.

Before the Sanhedrin

[53]They took Jesus to the high priest, and all the chief priests, elders and teachers of the law came together. [54]Peter followed him at a distance, right into

the courtyard of the high priest. There he sat with the guards and warmed himself at the fire.

[55]The chief priests and the whole Sanhedrin were looking for evidence against Jesus so that they could put him to death, but they did not find any. [56]Many testified falsely against him, but their statements did not agree.

[57]Then some stood up and gave this false testimony against him: [58]"We heard him say, 'I will destroy this man-made temple and in three days will build another, not made by man.'" [59]Yet even then their testimony did not agree.

[60]Then the high priest stood up before them and asked Jesus, "Are you not going to answer? What is this testimony that these men are bringing against you?" [61]But Jesus remained silent and gave no answer.

Again the high priest asked him, "Are you the Christ, the Son of the Blessed One?"

[62]"I am," said Jesus. "And you will see the Son of Man sitting at the right hand of the Mighty One and coming on the clouds of heaven."

[63]The high priest tore his clothes. "Why do we need any more witnesses?" he asked. [64]"You have heard the blasphemy. What do you think?"

They all condemned him as worthy of death. [65]Then some began to spit at him; they blindfolded him, struck him with their fists, and said, "Prophesy!" And the guards took him and beat him.

Peter Disowns Jesus

[66]While Peter was below in the courtyard, one of the servant girls of the high priest came by. [67]When she saw Peter warming himself, she looked closely at him.

"You also were with that Nazarene, Jesus," she said.

[68]But he denied it. "I don't know or understand what you're talking about," he said, and went out into the entryway.

[69]When the servant girl saw him there, she said again to those standing around, "This fellow is one of them." [70]Again he denied it.

After a little while, those standing near said to Peter, "Surely you are one of them, for you are a Galilean."

[71]He began to call down curses on himself, and he swore to them, "I don't know this man you're talking about."

[72]Immediately the rooster crowed the second time. Then Peter remembered the word Jesus had spoken to him: "Before the rooster crows twice you will disown me three times." And he broke down and wept.

Jesus Before Pilate

15 Very early in the morning, the chief priests, with the elders, the teachers of the law and the whole Sanhedrin, reached a decision. They bound Jesus, led him away and handed him over to Pilate.

²"Are you the king of the Jews?" asked Pilate.

"Yes, it is as you say," Jesus replied.

³The chief priests accused him of many things. ⁴So again Pilate asked him, "Aren't you going to answer? See how many things they are accusing you of."

⁵But Jesus still made no reply, and Pilate was amazed.

⁶Now it was the custom at the Feast to release a prisoner whom the people requested. ⁷A man called Barabbas was in prison with the insurrectionists who had committed murder in the uprising. ⁸The crowd came up and asked Pilate to do for them what he usually did.

⁹"Do you want me to release to you the king of the Jews?" asked Pilate, ¹⁰knowing it was out of envy that the chief priests had handed Jesus over to him. ¹¹But the chief priests stirred up the crowd to have Pilate release Barabbas instead.

¹²"What shall I do, then, with the one you call the king of the Jews?" Pilate asked them.

¹³"Crucify him!" they shouted.

¹⁴"Why? What crime has he committed?" asked Pilate.

But they shouted all the louder, "Crucify him!"

¹⁵Wanting to satisfy the crowd, Pilate released Barabbas to them. He had Jesus flogged, and handed him over to be crucified.

The Soldiers Mock Jesus

¹⁶The soldiers led Jesus away into the palace (that is, the Praetorium) and called together the whole company of soldiers. ¹⁷They put a purple robe on him, then twisted together a crown of thorns and set it on him. ¹⁸And they began to call out to him, "Hail, king of the Jews!" ¹⁹Again and again they struck him on the head with a staff and spit on him. Falling on their knees, they paid homage to him. ²⁰And when they had mocked him, they took off the purple robe and put his own clothes on him. Then they led him out to crucify him.

The Crucifixion

²¹A certain man from Cyrene, Simon, the father of Alexander and Rufus, was passing by on his way in from the country, and they forced him to carry the cross. ²²They brought Jesus to the place called Golgotha (which means The Place of the Skull). ²³Then they offered him wine mixed with myrrh, but he did not take it. ²⁴And they crucified him. Dividing up his clothes, they cast lots to see what each would get.

²⁵It was the third hour when they crucified him. ²⁶The written notice of the charge against him read: THE KING OF THE JEWS. ²⁷They crucified two robbers with him, one on his right and one on his left. ²⁹Those who passed by hurled insults at him, shaking their heads and saying, "So! You who are going to destroy the temple and build it in three days, ³⁰come down from the cross and save yourself!"

[31]In the same way the chief priests and the teachers of the law mocked him among themselves. "He saved others," they said, "but he can't save himself! [32]Let this Christ, this King of Israel, come down now from the cross, that we may see and believe." Those crucified with him also heaped insults on him.

The Death of Jesus

[33]At the sixth hour darkness came over the whole land until the ninth hour. [34]And at the ninth hour Jesus cried out in a loud voice, *"Eloi, Eloi, lama sabachthani?"*—which means, "My God, my God, why have you forsaken me?"

[35]When some of those standing near heard this, they said, "Listen, he's calling Elijah."

[36]One man ran, filled a sponge with wine vinegar, put it on a stick, and offered it to Jesus to drink. "Now leave him alone. Let's see if Elijah comes to take him down," he said.

[37]With a loud cry, Jesus breathed his last.

[38]The curtain of the temple was torn in two from top to bottom. [39]And when the centurion, who stood there in front of Jesus, heard his cry and saw how he died, he said, "Surely this man was the Son of God!"

[40]Some women were watching from a distance. Among them were Mary Magdalene, Mary the mother of James the younger and of Joses, and Salome. [41]In Galilee these women had followed him and cared for his needs. Many other women who had come up with him to Jerusalem were also there.

The Burial of Jesus

[42]It was Preparation Day (that is, the day before the Sabbath). So as evening approached, [43]Joseph of Arimathea, a prominent member of the Council, who was himself waiting for the kingdom of God, went boldly to Pilate and asked for Jesus' body. [44]Pilate was surprised to hear that he was already dead. Summoning the centurion, he asked him if Jesus had already died. [45]When he learned from the centurion that it was so, he gave the body to Joseph. [46]So Joseph bought some linen cloth, took down the body, wrapped it in the linen, and placed it in a tomb cut out of rock. Then he rolled a stone against the entrance of the tomb. [47]Mary Magdalene and Mary the mother of Joses saw where he was laid.

The Resurrection

16 When the Sabbath was over, Mary Magdalene, Mary the mother of James, and Salome bought spices so that they might go to anoint Jesus' body. [2]Very early on the first day of the week, just after sunrise, they were on their way to the tomb [3]and they asked each other, "Who will roll the stone away from the entrance of the tomb?"

⁴But when they looked up, they saw that the stone, which was very large, had been rolled away. ⁵As they entered the tomb, they saw a young man dressed in a white robe sitting on the right side, and they were alarmed.

⁶"Don't be alarmed," he said. "You are looking for Jesus the Nazarene, who was crucified. He has risen! He is not here. See the place where they laid him. ⁷But go, tell his disciples and Peter, 'He is going ahead of you into Galilee. There you will see him, just as he told you.'"

⁸Trembling and bewildered, the women went out and fled from the tomb. They said nothing to anyone, because they were afraid.

[The earliest manuscripts and some other ancient witnesses do not have Mark 16:9–20.]

⁹When Jesus rose early on the first day of the week, he appeared first to Mary Magdalene, out of whom he had driven seven demons. ¹⁰She went and told those who had been with him and who were mourning and weeping. ¹¹When they heard that Jesus was alive and that she had seen him, they did not believe it.

¹²Afterward Jesus appeared in a different form to two of them while they were walking in the country. ¹³These returned and reported it to the rest; but they did not believe them either.

¹⁴Later Jesus appeared to the Eleven as they were eating; he rebuked them for their lack of faith and their stubborn refusal to believe those who had seen him after he had risen.

¹⁵He said to them, "Go into all the world and preach the good news to all creation. ¹⁶Whoever believes and is baptized will be saved, but whoever does not believe will be condemned. ¹⁷And these signs will accompany those who believe: In my name they will drive out demons; they will speak in new tongues; ¹⁸they will pick up snakes with their hands; and when they drink deadly poison, it will not hurt them at all; they will place their hands on sick people, and they will get well."

¹⁹After the Lord Jesus had spoken to them, he was taken up into heaven and he sat at the right hand of God. ²⁰Then the disciples went out and preached everywhere, and the Lord worked with them and confirmed his word by the signs that accompanied it.

Endnotes

THE SEARCH

1. Look for a comprehensive list of these "coincidences" in a book titled *Universes*, by John Leslie (London: Routledge, 1989). Further reading: *God: The Evidence*, by Patrick Glynn, (Prima Publishing, 1997).

2. For much more on how modern archeology confirms much of the Bible, read *Is The Bible True?* by Jeffrey L. Sheler (HarperCollins Publishers, Inc., 1999).

3. The book I leaned on most is *The Life and Times of Jesus the Messiah*, by Alfred Eidersheim (Hendrickson Publishers, 1993). I highly recommend it, although it sometimes takes effort.

THE STORY

4. *The Carpenter's Cloth*, by Sigmund Brouwer. Copyright 1997 by J. Countryman, a division of Thomas Nelson, Inc. Used by permission of J. Countryman.

THE MEANING

5. John 20:6,7: "Then Simon Peter arrived and went inside. He also noticed the linen wrappings lying there, while the cloth that had covered Jesus' head was folded up and lying to the side."

Bibliography

Alexander, Pat, ed. *The Lion Handbook to the Bible*. Oxford, England: Lion Publishing, 1973.

Barclay, William. *The Gospel of Mark*. Philadelphia: The Westminster Press, 1975.

———. *The Gospel of Matthew, Volume I*. Philadelphia: The Westminster Press, 1975.

Beers, V. Gilbert. *The Book of Life*. Elgin: Books For Living, Inc., 1980.

Connolly, Peter. *Living In The Time of Jesus of Nazareth*. Oxford, England: Oxford University Press, 1983.

Edersheim, Alfred. *The Life and Times of Jesus the Messiah*: Hendrickson Publishers, Inc., 1993.

Glynn, Patrick. *GOD: The Evidence*. Prima Publishing, 1997.

Johnson, Luke Timothy. *The Real Jesus*. Harper San Francisco, 1995.

Kreeft, Peter. *Socrates Meets Jesus*. InterVarsity Press, IL: 1987.

Maier, Paul L. *Pontius Pilate*. Grand Rapids: Kregel, 1968.

Pixner, Bargil, O.S.B. *With Jesus Through Galilee According to the Fifth Gospel*. Rosh Pina, Israel: Corazin Publishing, 1992.

Pritchard, James B. *Master, A Life of Jesus*. Wheaton: Victor Books, 1984.

Richman, Chaim. *The Holy Temple of Jerusalem*. Jerusalem, Israel: Cartam, The Israel Map and Publishing Company, 1997.

Sobol, Dava. *Galileo's Daughter*. New York: Viking, 1999.

Spoto, Donald. *The Hidden Jesus*. New York: St. Martin's Press, 1998.

Ward, Kaari, ed. *Jesus and His Times*. Pleasantville: Reader's Digest General Books, 1987.

Wilkinson, John. *The Jerusalem Jesus Knew*. Thomas Nelson, Inc., 1983.

Whiston, William, translator. *The Complete Works of Josephus*. Grand Rapids: Kregel Publications, 1960.

Yancey, Philip. *The Jesus I Never Knew*. Grand Rapids: Zondervan Publishing House, 1995.